PROFESSOR M.S.RAO, Ph.D.

INTERNATIONAL LEADERSHIP GURU

M.GANESH SAI

SOAR LIKE EAGLES!
SUCCESS TOOLS FOR FRESHERS

FOREWORD BY
JOHN H. ZENGER

Soar like Eagles! Success Tools for Freshers
M.S. Rao and M. Ganesh Sai

© 2014, *Author*

All rights reserved,

Published by :

BSP BS Publications

A unit of **BSP Books Pvt. Ltd.**
4-4-309, Giriraj Lane, Sultan Bazar,
Hyderabad - 500 095 - A.P.
Phone : 040 - 23445605, 23445688
e-mail : info@bspbooks.net
www.bspublications.net

ISBN: 978-93-90211-11-1

International Acclaim for this Book!

"While his ostensible focus is on "freshers" (those just entering the workforce), Professor M. S. Rao and M. Ganesh Sai remind us that we are all students, and that we can and should continue to hone our communication, team building and problem solving skills throughout our careers and our lives. With these skills, we will surely *Soar Like Eagles!*"

Marshall Goldsmith
The Thinkers50 Award Winner (sponsored by Harvard Business Review) for Most-Influential Leadership Thinker in the World

---

"Your ability to get the right first job for you can have an impact on the rest of your career. This book shows you how to start your career in the best possible way."

Brian Tracy
Author – Get Paid More and Promoted Faster

"Professor M.S. Rao and his son M. Ganesh Sai have come out with yet another inspiring leadership book for students, *Soar Like Eagles! Success Tools for Freshers* (For those who are not familiar - In India, "freshers" means the fresh graduates passing out of educational institutions seeking employment opportunities in the corporate world). This book contains interesting anecdotes, illustrations and stories for freshers to grab the employment opportunities and fast-track their careers. It is an inspiring book every fresher should read!"

Dr. Tony Alessandra
Author of The Platinum Rule and Charisma and CEO of
www.Assessments24x7.com

"The international management thinker, Professor M.S.Rao with his son M.Ganesh Sai authored the book titled *Soar Like Eagles! Success Tools for Freshers* It equips freshers and students with tools and techniques and builds their confidence to achieve big in their lives."

Chris Widener
Bestselling leadership author
www.ChrisWIdener.com

"The global leadership guru, Professor M.S. Rao with his son, M. Ganesh Sai have come out with yet another leadership book for students. It outlines the roadmap for students' success and elaborates various aspects of education, employment and emotional intelligence to achieve quick career success."

Arthur F. Carmazzi
World's Top Ten Leadership Guru and Founder of Directive Communication Psychology
Author of "Lessons from the Monkey King – Leading Change to Create Gorilla Sized Results

---

"This book encourages freshers and leaders across the social order, to pursue excellence in everything they do, even the small stuff. It shapes in the mind of readers, constructive impressions that engage intelligence with heart, responsibility with expertise. It's a plan you will value considering."

Rob Clarke
Founder, LearnX Foundation

"International leadership educator and speaker, Professor M.S. Rao co-authored another inspiring leadership book for students with his son M.Ganesh Sai. *Soar Like Eagles! Success Tools for Freshers* is a book I strongly recommend. It is clear the Professor Rao and his son are passionate about students and they beseech students to add value to soar like eagles; and urge educators to help successful students become even more successful."

Terri Levine, PhD
The Business Mentoring Expert
Bestselling Author of 'Coaching is for Everyone'

"Professor M.S.Rao is one of the world's leading leadership consultants, coaches, and speakers with 32 years of experience and has published a new book with his son M. Ganesh Sai *Soar Like Eagles! Success Tools for Freshers* This inspirational book covers several important topics: Roadmap for students' success, various aspects of education, employment and emotional intelligence, the 'Play and Learn' method - an innovative learning tool, concerns of new graduates and equips them with clarifications, adding value and help them soar like eagles, fires up educators to help successful students to become even more successful. This book is written in a very clear and understandable style as we are used to expect from Professor M.S.Rao. We can feel Professor M.S.Rao's enthusiasm for the subject matter and sharing his knowledge. Highly recommended."

Dr. James Wang
American Institute of Business Psychology,
www.aiobp.org

Quotes

"When I asked God for strength, He gave me difficult situations to face. When I asked God for brain and brawn, He gave me puzzles in life to solve. When I asked God for happiness, He showed me some unhappy people. When I asked God for wealth, He showed me how to work hard. When I asked God for favors, He showed me opportunities to work hard. When I asked God for peace, He showed me how to help others. God Gave me nothing I wanted, He gave me everything I needed."

– Swami Vivekananda

"Keep your dreams alive. Understand to achieve anything requires faith and belief in yourself, vision, hard work, determination, and dedication. Remember all things are possible for those who believe."

– Gail Devers

"You can be anything you want to be, if only you believe with sufficient conviction and act in accordance with your faith; for whatever the mind can conceive and believe, the mind can achieve."

– Napoleon Hill

"Finish each day and be done with it. You have done what you could; some blunders and absurdities have crept in; forget them as soon as you can. Tomorrow is a new day; you shall begin it serenely and with too high a spirit to be encumbered with your old nonsense."

– Ralph Waldo Emerson

"Dreams have only one owner at a time. That's why dreamers are lonely."

– Erma Bombeck, author

"The subconscious mind makes no distinction between constructive and destructive thought impulses. It works with the material we feed it, through our thought impulses. The sub-conscious mind will translate into reality a thought driven by fear, just as readily as it will translate into reality a thought driven by courage or faith."

– Napoleon Hill

"The state of your life is nothing more than a reflection of your state of mind."

– Dr. Wayne W. Dyer

"Your own mind is a sacred enclosure into which nothing harmful can enter except by your promotion."

– Ralph Waldo Emerson

"Men are not prisoners of fate, but only prisoners of their own minds."

– Franklin Roosevelt

"The human mind is like umbrella. It functions best when open."

– Max Gropius

"Motivation is life food for the brain. You cannot get enough in one sitting. It needs continual and regular top up's."

– Peter Davies

"You have brains in your head. You have feet in your shoes. You can steer yourself in any direction you choose. You're on your own. And you know what you know. You are the guy who'll decide where to go."

– Theodor Seuss Geisel

"To many a man, and sometimes to a youth, there comes the opportunity to choose between honorable competence and tainted wealth. The young man who starts out to be poor and honorable, holds in his hand one of the strongest elements of success."

– Orison Swett Marden

"Goals. There's no telling what you can do when you get inspired by them. There's no telling what you can do when you believe in them. And there's no telling what will happen when you act upon them."

– Jim Rohn

"If you want to reach a goal, you must 'see the reaching' in your own mind before you actually arrive at your goal."

– Zig Ziglar

"The reason most people never reach their goals is that they don't define them, learn about them or even seriously consider them as believable or achievable. Winners can tell you where they are going, what they plan to do along the way, and who will be sharing the adventure with them."

– Denis Waitley

"A dream is just a dream. A goal is a dream with a plan and a deadline."

– Harvey Mackay

"Obstacles are those frightful things you see when you take your eyes off your goal."

– Henry Ford

"All men dream: but not equally. Those who dream by night in the dusty recesses of their minds wake in the day to find that it was vanity: but the dreamers of the day are dangerous men, for they may act their dreams with open eyes, to make it possible."

– T.E. Lawrence

"I had to make my own living and my own opportunity! But I made it! Don't sit down and wait for the opportunities to come. Get up and make them!"

– C.J. Walker

"The important thing is not being afraid to take a chance. Remember, the greatest failure is to not try. Once you find something you love to do, be the best at doing it."

– Debbi Fields

"The supreme quality for leadership is unquestionably integrity. Without it, no real success is possible, no matter whether it is on a section gang, a football field, in an army, or in an office."

– Dwight D. Eisenhower

"The function of leadership is to produce more leaders, not more followers."

– Ralph Nader

"Leadership is based on inspiration, not domination; on cooperation, not intimidation."

– William Arthur Ward

"Teachers open the door. You enter by yourself."

– Chinese saying

"Better than a thousand days of diligent study is one day with a great teacher."

– Japanese Proverb

"It is the supreme art of the teacher to awaken joy in creative expression and knowledge."

– Albert Einstein

"Big egos have little ears."

– Robert Schuller

"Look for intelligence and judgment and, most critically, a capacity to anticipate, to see around corners. Also look for loyalty, integrity, a high energy drive, a balanced ego and the drive to get things done."

– Colin Powell

"Any genuine teaching will result, if successful, in someone's knowing how to bring about a better condition of things than existed earlier."

– John Dewey

"Teaching is the profession that teaches all the other professions"

– Anonymous

"The mediocre teacher tells. The good teacher explains. The superior teacher demonstrates. The great teacher inspires."

– William Arthur Ward

"Good teaching is more a giving of right questions than a giving of right answers."

– Josef Albers

"The leaders who work most effectively, it seems to me, never say "I." And that's not because they have trained themselves not to say "I." They don't think "I." They think "we"; they think "team." They understand their job to be to make the team function. They accept responsibility and don't sidestep it, but "we" gets the credit…. This is what creates trust, what enables you to get the task done."

– Peter Drucker

"It's too bad failures don't give seminars. Wouldn't that be valuable? If you meet a guy who has messed up his life for forty years, you've just got to say, 'John, if I bring my   journal and promise to take good notes, would you spend a day with me?'"

– Jim Rohn

"Writing is the only thing that, when I do it, I don't feel I should be doing something else."

– Gloria Steimen

"You don't concentrate on risks. You concentrate on results. No risk is too great to prevent the necessary job from getting done."

– Chuck Yeager

"Time = Life. Master your time and master your life."

– Alan Lakein

"I can tell how much money you make by looking at how you respect your time."

– Mike Litman

"Until we can manage TIME, we can manage nothing else."

– Peter F. Drucker

"The quality of life is the quality of your time management."

– Brian Tracy

"When you kill time, you kill your opportunities for success."

– Denis Waitley

"Time is the most valuable thing a man can spend."

– Theophrastus

"It's how we spend our time here and now, that really matters. If you are fed up with the way you have come to interact with time, change it."

– Marcia Wieder

"Realize that now, in this moment of time, you are creating. You are creating your next moment. That is what's real."

– Sara Paddison

"A man who dares to waste one hour of time has not discovered the value of life."

– Charles Darwin

"There are three constants in life... change, choice and principles."

– Stephen Covey

"Opportunity often comes disguised in the form of misfortune, or temporary defeat"

– Napoleon Hill

"The secret of success in life is for a person to be ready for opportunity when it comes."

– Benjamin Disraeli

"Your work is to discover your work and then with all your heart to give yourself to it."

– Buddha

"You cannot speak that which you do not know. You cannot share that which you do not feel. You cannot translate that which you do not have. And you cannot give that which you do not possess. To give it and to share it, and for it to be effective, you first need to have it. Good communication starts with good preparation."

– Jim Rohn

"Success consists of going from failure to failure without loss of enthusiasm."

– Winston Churchill

"Big goals get big results. No goals get no results or somebody else's results."

– Mark Victor Hansen

"A winner is someone who recognizes his God-given talents, works his tail off to develop them into skills, and uses these skills to accomplish his goals."

- Larry Bird

"A dream you dream alone is only a dream. A dream you dream together is reality."

– John Lennon

"Leaders are made, not born. You learn to become a leader by doing what other excellent leaders have done before you. You become proficient in your job or skill, and then you become proficient at understanding the motivations and behaviors of other people."

– Brian Tracy

"Leadership cannot really be taught. It can only be learned."

– Harold Geneen

"The art of communication is the language of leadership."

– James Humes

"Good communication does not mean that you have to speak in perfectly formed sentences and paragraphs. It isn't about slickness. Simple and clear go a long way."

– John Kotter

"Associate with well-mannered persons and your manners will improve. Run around with decent folk and your own decent instincts will be strengthened."

– Stanley Walker

"Nothing is less important than which fork you use. Etiquette is the science of living. It embraces everything. It is ethics. It is honor."

– Emily Post

"When a team outgrows individual performance and learns team confidence, excellence becomes a reality."

– Joe Paterno

"Strive for excellence, not perfection."

– H. Jackson Brown Jr.

"If you are going to achieve excellence in big things, you develop the habit in little matters. Excellence is not an exception, it is a prevailing attitude."

– Colin Powell

"If what you are getting online is for free, you are not the customer, you are the product."

– Jonathan Zittrain, Professor of Internet Law

"Education does not take place when you learn something you did not know before. Education is your ability to use what you have learned to be better today than you were yesterday."

– Iyanla Vanzant

"It is impossible for a man to learn what he thinks he already knows."

– Epictetus

"The goal of education is the advancement of knowledge and the dissemination of truth."

– John F. Kennedy

"I have so much admiration for women who are mothers, who balance family and work."

– Beyonce

"Don't confuse having a career with having a life."

– Hillary Clinton

"Leadership, like coaching, is fighting for the hearts and souls of men and getting them to believe in you."

– Eddie Robinson

"Coaching is unlocking a person's potential to maximize their own performance. It is helping them to learn rather than teaching them."

– Timothy Gallwey

"Who exactly seeks out a coach? Winners who want even more out of life."

– Chicago Tribune

"Coaching: To get people to do what they don't want to do in order to achieve what they want to achieve."

– Tom Landry

"Coaching is the quickest, most customized, and most powerful behavior change technique available to a leader."

– David B. Peterson

"When you study great teachers... you will learn much more from their caring and hard work than from their style."

– William Glasser

"I am indebted to my father for living, but to my teacher for living well"

– Alexander, The Great

"Example has more followers than reason. We unconsciously imitate what pleases us, and approximate to the characters we most admire."

– Christian Nevell Bovee

"I start with the premise that the function of leadership is to produce more leaders, not more followers."

– Ralph Nader

"Leaders don't create followers, they create more leaders."

– Tom Peters

"Life is the sum of all your choices."

– Albert Camus

"The hardest thing to learn in life is which bridge to cross and which to burn."

– David Russell

"Everyone is necessarily the hero of his own life story."

– John Barth

"You must have control of the authorship of your own destiny. The pen that writes your life story must be held in your own hand."

– Irene C. Kassorla

"Life is like a blanket too short. You pull it up and your toes rebel, you yank it down and shivers meander about your shoulder; but cheerful folks manage to draw their knees up and pass a very comfortable night."

– Marion Howard

"Life: It is about the gift not the package it comes in."

– Dennis P. Costea Jr.

"Do what best you can do today thinking that there is no tomorrow. While learning think that you live longer and while sharing knowledge think that today is the last day in life. You will never be happy if you continue to search for what happiness consists of. You will never live if you are looking for the meaning of life."

– Albert Camus

"We're all accidental soldiers in the army of life."

– Terri Guillemets

"Life can be easy, it is only question of choosing between solutions and illusions."

– Didier D'haese

"Maxim for life: You get treated in life the way you teach people to treat you."

– Wayne Dyer

"Never get so busy making a living that you forget to make a life."

– Paula Williams, British designer, publisher

"Perhaps our eyes need to be washed by our tears once in a while, so that we can see life with a clearer view again."

– Alex Tan

"Life is pleasant. Death is peaceful. It's the transition that's troublesome."

– Isaac Asimov

"But there is suffering in life, and there are defeats. No one can avoid them. But it's better to lose some of the battles in the struggles for your dreams than to be defeated without ever knowing what you're fighting for."

– Paulo Coelho

"Ultimately, man should not ask what the meaning of his life is, but rather he must recognize that it is he who is asked."

– Viktor E. Frankl

"What counts in life is not the mere fact that we have lived. It is what difference we have made to the lives of others that will determine the significance of the life we lead."

– Nelson Mandela, Former President of South Africa

"If I, being a mother of two, can win a medal, so can you all. Take me as an example and don`t give up".

– Mary Kom, Winner of Bronze Medal for Boxing for India

"Challenges are easier to overcome if you can remain focused on the desired results."

– Tony Richards

"A man does what he must... in spite of personal consequences, in spite of obstacles and dangers, and pressures... and that is the basis of all human morality."

– John F. Kennedy

"It is a paradoxical but profoundly true and important principle of life that the most likely way to reach a goal is to be aiming not at that goal itself but at some more ambitious goal beyond it."

– Arnold Toynbee

"No leader can possibly have all the answers …. The actual solutions about how best to meet the challenges of the moment have to be made by the people closest to the action……The leader has to find the way to empower those frontline people, to challenge them, to provide them with the resources they need, and then to hold them accountable. As they struggle with…this challenge, the leader becomes their coach, teacher, and facilitator. Change how you define leadership, and you change how you run a company."

– Steve Miller, Group Managing Director, Royal Dutch/Shell.

"In a day, when you don't come across any problems, then you can be sure that you are traveling in the wrong path…"

– John F. Kennedy

"Failure is only postponed success as long as courage coaches ambition. The habit of persistence is the habit of victory."

– Herbert Kaufman

"Ambition is like hunger; it obeys no law but its appetite."

– Josh Billings, columnist and humorist

"Character cannot be developed in ease and quiet. Only through experiences of trial and suffering can the soul be strengthened, vision cleared, ambition inspired and success achieved."

– Helen Keller

"The difference between a job and a career is the difference between forty and sixty hours a week."

– Robert Frost

"Everything tells me that I am about to make a wrong decision, but making mistakes is just part of life. What does the world want of me? Does it want me to take no risks, to go back to where I came from because I didn't have the courage to say "yes" to life?"

– Paulo Coelho, Eleven Minutes

"Cheerfulness and contentment are great beautifiers and are famous preservers of youthful looks."

– Charles Dickens, novelist

"Weakness of attitude becomes weakness of character."

– Albert Einstein

"Education is the most powerful weapon which you can use to change the world."

– Nelson Mandela

"What sculpture is to a block of marble, education is to the human soul."

– Joseph Addison

"Make me the master of education, and I will undertake to change the world."

– Gottfried Wilhelm Leibnitz

"Education is a weapon, whose effect depends on who holds it in his hands and at whom it is aimed."

– Joseph Stalin

"Better to remain silent and be thought a fool then to speak out and remove all doubt."

– Abraham Lincoln

"Nearly all men can stand adversity, but if you want to test a man's character, give him power."

– Abraham Lincoln

"With malice toward none, with charity for all, with firmness in the right, as God gives us to see the right, let us strive on to finish the work we are in, to bind up the nation's wounds."

– Abraham Lincoln

"If you wish to achieve worthwhile things in your personal and career life, you must become a worthwhile person in your own self-development."

– Brian Tracy

"Today, many companies are reporting that their number one constraint on growth is the inability to hire workers with the necessary skills."

– Bill Clinton

"It is the capacity to develop and improve their skills that distinguishes leaders from followers."

– Warren Bennis and Burt Nanus

"Knowledge is gained by learning; trust by doubt; skill by practice; and love by love."

– Thomas S Szasz

"Skill without imagination is craftsmanship and gives us many useful objects such as wickerwork picnic baskets. Imagination without skill gives us modern art."

– Tom Stoppard

"Because introverts are typically good listeners and, at least, have the appearance of calmness, we are attractive to emotionally needy people. Introverts, gratified that other people are initiating with them, can easily get caught in these exhausting and unsatisfying relationships."

– Adam S. McHugh

"Nature teaches more than she preaches. There are no sermons in stones. It is easier to get a spark out of a stone than a moral."

– John Burroughs

"I am a leader by default, only because nature does not allow a vacuum."

– Desmond Tutu

"Man is fully responsible for his nature and choices"

– Jean-Paul Sartre

"When you hire people who are smarter than you are, you prove you are smarter than they are."

– R.H. Grant

"The adventure of life is to learn. The purpose of life is to grow. The nature of life is to change. The challenge of life is to overcome. The essence of life is to care. The opportunity of life is to serve. The secret of life is to dare. The spice of life is to befriend. The beauty of life is to give."

– William Arthur Ward

"A brain is a society of very small, simple modules that cannot be said to be thinking, that are not smart in themselves. But when you have a network of them together, out of that arises a kind of smartness."

– Kevin Kelly

"A man must be big enough to admit his mistakes, smart enough to profit from them, and strong enough to correct them."

– John C. Maxwell

"We make a living by what we get, but we make a life by what we give."

– Winston Churchill

"I'm convinced that we can write and live our own scripts more than most people will acknowledge. I also know the price that must be paid. It's a real struggle to do it. It requires visualization and affirmation. It involves living a life of integrity, starting with making and keeping promises, until the whole human personality, the senses, the thinking, the feeling, and the intuition are ultimately integrated and harmonized."

– Stephen R. Covey

Dedication

Dedicated to M. Padmavathy, the angel of our home; and M. Ramakrishna Sayee, pearl of our home.

Foreword

My Father was a classic "self-made" man. He grew up in a home with very little material possessions and as the oldest son, he worked to help support his family. Unable to attend college, he nevertheless became a highly educated man through a great deal of self-study. As I looked over his library that he built as a very young man, I noticed a book titled, *Pushing to the Front*, by Orison Swett Marden. I later learned that it was the first of the motivational, self-help books that influenced many people's lives. Well known people who gave credit to it for their personal inspiration included Henry Ford, Harvey Firestone, J.P. Morgan and Thomas Edison. My Father frequently referred to the influence the book had been on him.

Professor M. S. Rao's book, coauthored with his son, M. Ganesh Sai strikes me as just such a book. It is one more volume of practical wisdom, distilled from their personal experience and enriched by ideas gleaned from countless other thought leaders, social scientists and philosophers. They have compiled and organized these thoughts in such a way as to make them highly accessible. They have geared them to the young person who is a student, and these ideas will be particularly useful in those highly formative years.

From any one of the forty chapters, the reader should be able to glean some piece of wisdom that will help to guide them on their path to greater success.   Because of that, this book will probably find its way on to many bookshelves, and in years to come the children or grandchildren of the original reader will learn that this was the book that inspired their ancestor to greatness.

John H. Zenger
CEO
Zenger Folkman
www.zengerfolkman.com

Preface

"We become what we think about all day long."
– RALPH WALDO EMERSON

Welcome to *Soar Like Eagles! Success Tools for Freshers.* You may be wondering why we are doing another book on students' success as we often author books on leadership. We are passionate about students and their success. We want to equip them with tools and techniques to achieve success and fast-track their careers. This book stands out from our other books at it emphasizes on the concerns of freshers who have a number of myths about their careers and corporate life. The book debunks the myths and enlightens them with right inputs about the expectations of the employers and the skills the latter look for in freshers. Hence, we authored this book exclusively for students to address their concerns.

The book is divided into three parts. Part I begins with a call to lead India as the future of India depends on students. It reminds them about their hidden power and potential. It is essential to develop an ambitious mindset to soar like eagles. It compares success with chess and unfolds three aspects to achieve success. It unveils Sigmund Freud's Id, Ego and Super Ego and advises to set goals. It urges to spot talents and build skills around them; and outlines the skills expected by employers from freshers.

Employers hire for attitude and train for skills. Hence, it is essential to build your attitude to enhance employability and achieve all-round success. It equips freshers with eight habits outlined by Stephen R Covey. It describes the importance of soft and hard skills among freshers and advices them to blend both to excel as smart leaders. It implores to acquire inquisitiveness, manage time and work within the companies for a longer time to fast-track their careers. It advises students to stay away from suicidal tendencies; build brand image; enhance fan base; and make peace to progress.

Part II differentiates between education and experience. It enlightens that education is not for employment alone but for empowerment and enlightenment. Education includes curricular and extracurricular activities. It eulogizes the role of S. Radhakrishan, former President of India who was a great teacher. It implores educators to be responsible and compares them with Lord Shri Krishna who was a great coach. It is essential for educators to develop emotional intelligence and calls upon them to help successful students become even more successful.

Part III investigates unsuccessful parents and their successful children. It reveals that women appreciate men who are persistent by nature. It appeals all to respect women as we all were born from the wombs of women. It concludes with a clarion call to students to add value to themselves, parents and nation as a whole.

The book contains Appendix A - A test that helps you find out whether you are a left-brainer or a right-brainer; Appendix B - 'Play and Learn' method which is an innovative learning tool;

and Appendix C debunks several career and corporate myths freshers have, and clarifies their concerns to build confidence in them.

We hope this book will inspire you to make it a priority, learn as much as you can, commit time and attention to acquire tools and techniques needed for your career success, happiness and peace.

Professor M.S.Rao
M. Ganesh Sai

Acknowledgments

Writing a book is never a solo project. We are deeply indebted to many people whose expertise, wisdom, and encouragement kept us going.

Several quotes, examples and anecdotes are the result of a collection from different sources. It is practically impossible to acknowledge to each one of them separately. While we have tried to give credit wherever it is due, in case if we have missed anything, we will give due credit in future editions if it is brought to our notice.

We thank everyone including the team of B.S. Publications for publication of this book. We specifically thank Nikhil Shah and Anil Shah for their initiative, positive attitude, and professionalism in publication of this book.

We express special thanks to all the readers who graciously took time off from their busy schedules to write to us, and share their views, and offer feedback on our books

21 Success Sutras for Leaders

Smart Leadership: Lessons for Leaders

Secrets of Your Leadership Success: The 11 Indispensable E's of a Leader

Soft Leadership: Make Others Feel More Important

Success Can Be Yours

Stand Out! Build a Successful Career and Become a Global Leader

Sharpen Your Mind: Acquire Tools to Achieve Your Success

Strategies for Improving Your Business Communication: The Book for Leaders to Communicate and Achieve Professional Success

Sage Advice for Students and Educators: Stay Inspired!

Soup for Academic Leaders: Acquire Teaching Tools to Achieve Your Academic Leadership Success

Spirit of Indian Youth: Soft Skills for Young Managers

Smartness Guide: Success Tools for Students

Spot Your Leadership Style: Build Your Leadership Brand

Secrets for Success: Failure is only a Comma, Not a Full Stop

Soft Skills: Enhancing Employability

Soft Skills for Students: Classroom to Corporate

We wholeheartedly thank you for your endless support and love.

Contents

Soar Like Eagles! Success Tools for Freshers

PART I - STUDENTS

PART II - EDUCATORS

STUDENTS

CHAPTER 1

Lead India

*"Do not follow where the path may lead. Go instead where there
is no path and leave a trail."*
– MURIEL STRODE

Welcome to *Soar Like Eagles! Success Tools for Freshers.* We
have authored this book to offer success tools for students and
freshers and eulogize the role of educators who help successful
students become even more successful. From our experience
and observation, we found that students and especially freshers
having several myths about career and corporate life. They
have several concerns and we clarify them in this book to
enhance their employability and fast-track their careers.

Lead India

Whenever I interact with students I find tons of fire and passion
among them. Most of them are concerned about the future of
India, and are upset the way things are happening around in
our country. They are upset with the political system and the
way corruption has entered into all spheres. In fact, corruption
has become a cancer to Indian society. Students often ask me
how to change the system and how to make our country a

prosperous one, and how to keep it on the top of the global map. I am equally concerned as I am passionate about Indian students and my country. That is the reason why I chose teaching as a profession out of my passion to groom students as responsible citizens and leaders so that they can lead our country successfully and make it as a Super Power in future.

When you want to bring out the desired changes in the system you must set up an organization that can voice the people's opinions. You must come out with a common cause that concerns the people; and influence interested people to join in your team. Meet regularly at a venue to raise the issues concerning the people and bring awareness through various unconventional means and methods. You can make use of social media to reach out to the people. Invite celebrities who have passion to make a difference in the lives of people, and ask them to deliver lectures regularly. Over a period of time, you can build a mass movement to bring out the change in the society. It is like a ripple effect. When you throw a stone into water it takes time for the waves to reach the shore. Similarly, when you start such organization it takes time and you find a number of challenges on your path. You must overcome all these challenges from time to time by staying motivated and aligning all your energies and efforts in the desired direction. Over a period of time, you will find change in the mindset of the people; they will respect your initiative; and will become a part of your successful team to transform the society.

Remember, the day the corruption enters into armed forces and educational institutions the country will collapse. Therefore, ensure that the cancer of corruption doesn't creep into Indian Armed Forces and educational institutions. Take initiative and work towards bringing out the change the way you want because the future of our country lies in your hands. It is your responsibility to hand over better society to your next generation. Remember the inspiring words of Margaret Mead, "Never doubt that a small group of thoughtful, committed citizens can change the world; indeed, it's the only thing that ever has."

We will discuss success tools for students in the following chapters.

> *"If your actions inspire others to dream more, learn more, do more and become more, you are a leader."*
>
> – JOHN QUINCY ADAMS

References

http://www.facebook.com/pages/Professor-MSRao/451516514937414?skip_nax_wizard=true

http://speakermix.com/professor-m-s-rao

Author's Blogs:

http://professormsraoguru.blogspot.com

http://professormsrao.blogspot.com

http://profmsr.blogspot.com

CHAPTER 2

Power of Students

"The error of youth is to believe that intelligence is a substitute for experience, while the error of age is to believe experience is a substitute for intelligence."
- ERNEST HEMINGWAY

In one of my soft skills training programs, a participant asked why the youth in India are not encouraged to lead the country. I thought for a moment and replied as follows:

Leadership is not the privilege of the few. Anybody can lead the country as long as there is fire in them to lead and a heart to make a difference in the lives of people. Indian culture and mindset is different from rest of the world. We in India respect the elderly and experienced people. These people have seen the life and faced several challenges and can take more precautions to minimize mistakes and maximize leadership effectiveness. These are some of the reasons why the aged and experienced people lead the country in India. At the same time the old people have regimented thoughts and are hardwired with conventional thinking with traditional approach which proves to be ineffective sometimes.

When we look at young people, we realize that they have tons of fire and passion to lead this country but don't have any experience. Most of the times they do good as they don't have any inhibitions but sometimes commit mistakes that prove to be costly for the country. When we look holistically the youth are very powerful. We cannot underestimate their intelligence, competencies and capabilities. When you look at Mark Zuckerberg who by launching the Facebook, became a trendsetter and demonstrated that students can achieve anything and everything if only they are determined. He has been listed as the youngest billionaire CEO in the Fortune 500 companies. Similarly, Michael Dell the founder of Dell, and the founders of Google to name a few have started at a young age and excelled as successful entrepreneurs. They were students whose dreams began on the educational institutions.   This shows the power of students. The present day students are much more powerful and are highly ambitious than their predecessors. They are quick thinkers and learners, backed by technological bent of mind.

While old people follow the trend, young people set the trend. Both have merits and demerits. But when we want our country to progress quickly we need young people to lead this country. Even if they make mistakes they can correct themselves and bounce back and take the country forward by learning lessons from their failures as age is in their favor. Hence, more youth must participate to lead our country in the near future to take our nation to glory.

"The young do not know enough to be prudent, and therefore they attempt the impossible - and achieve it, generation after generation."

- PEARL S. BUCK

CHAPTER 3

Cultivate an Ambitious Mindset

"A man's worth is no greater than the worth of his ambitions."
- MARCUS AURELIUS ANTONINUS,
FORMER ROMAN EMPEROR

Students must learn how to set ambitious mindset to achieve success in their lives. It is always good to be ambitious to stand out from others and great to accomplish goals to soar like an eagle. In fact, to aim low is a crime. Here goes the story of two masons:

A Tale of Two Masons

Two masons were working for construction of a flyover in a city. A passerby asked them what they were doing. One mason replied that he was constructing a wall while another mason replied that he was busy constructing a great flyover in the city. Although both were busy with their work one mason had an average mindset of constructing a wall in his mind while the another mason had great mindset of constructing a flyover in his mind, and he displayed a lot of pride for being a part of the prestigious project by radiating passion towards his work. From this story, it is obvious that although people do the same work some think small while some think big due to their mindsets. Those who think big develop ambitious mindset and achieve greatness in their lives.

Set an Ambitious Mindset

To set an ambitious mindset, you must think big and be passionate in your area of interest. You must create an environment where you can grow rapidly in your life. Mark Twain rightly said, "Keep away from people who try to belittle your ambitions. Small people always do that, but the really great make you feel that you, too, can become great." Hence, stay away from negative people who invalidate you and poison your mind with negative inputs. You must create a network of good people to maintain it. You must acquire knowledge accordingly. You must come out of your comfort zone and reset your goals after accomplishing your goals. You must work hard and raise your bar constantly. You must learn, unlearn and relearn to stay relevant. You must constantly fuel your goals. Above all, set your inner dialogue with audacious goals and fuel them constantly with needed inputs. Your actions and behavior will change accordingly, and over a period of time you find yourself possessing ambitious mindset.

Ambitious Leadership

Ambition is an integral part of leadership. Leaders can channel their ambition either for good or bad. In fact, ambition is a double edged sword. It is both a vice and virtue. You can use it either for good or bad. For instance, leader like Huey Long, the Governor of Louisiana in the Thirties improved the state's infrastructure through public works, but he achieved his goals through ruthless and corrupt means. Being ambitious is not bad, but how implement it is more important. If you emphasize on right means to achieve your goals, being ambitious is good. In contrast, if you emphasize on wrong means to achieve your ends, being ambitious is bad. Edmund Burke, the 18th century political theorist rightly said, "Ambition can creep as well as soar."

Reasons for Failures

Sometimes people fail to stick to their ambitious mindsets after cultivating it due to various reasons. In fact, there are two types of threats – internal and external. Some people deviate from their goals and enter into unfocused areas that prove to be very detrimental at the end. This is known as internal threat. Sometimes people may not be able to focus on their goals due to unexpected external distractions. This is known as external threat, and it is tough to predict. In fact, most of the people fail due to external threats rather than internal threats. Hence, you must align constantly by focusing on your goals, and be on the chosen track by taking remedial actions to accomplish your goals. Remember the Chinese proverb, "An ambitious horse will never return to its old stable." To conclude, students must always think big, set goals accordingly and work with passion and perseverance to become great in their lives.

> *"Ambition has one heel nailed in well, though she stretch her fingers to touch the heavens."*
>
> - LAO TZU

Reference

Leadership: Ambition--Vice or Virtue? By John Baldoni

CHAPTER 4

Don't Compare with Others

*"When you are content to be simply yourself and don't compare
or compete, everybody will respect you."*
- LAO TZU

People often compare with others. They compare themselves with Bill Gates, Richard Branson, Barack Obama and other successful personalities. They underestimate themselves and rarely think of their hidden potential. At times, it leads to dissatisfaction and depression. Sometimes they expect more than what they want without weighing at the pros and cons. Here goes the story of a beautiful horse that wanted to be something else:

Once there was a beautiful horse. It wanted to look more attractive and beautiful. It often felt bad that its legs were fat and neck was small. Hence, it prayed to God to gift with a long neck and lean legs. God advised the horse to reconsider the request. The horse was adamant and determined to have the desired appearance with features and stood by its request. God blessed with the boon and horse looked like a camel with long neck and lean legs. It felt very bad but could not help. In our real lives too, people are not happy with what they have and they still crave for more by comparing with others.

God created you with some purpose and special appearance. Don't try to become somebody else. Alen Strike rightly said, "Don't compare yourself with anyone in this world. If you do so, you are insulting yourself." Besides, people often confuse comparison with inspiration as both are different. You can take inspiration from others but you cannot compare with others. Remember that God blessed you with unique strengths, skills, and abilities. Hence, be yourself and stand out!

> *"Everyone has his own specific vocation or mission in life; everyone must carry out a concrete assignment that demands fulfillment. Therein he cannot be replaced, nor can his life be repeated, thus, everyone's task is unique as his specific opportunity to implement it."*
>
> — VIKTOR E. FRANKL

CHAPTER 5

Chess and Success

*"Success isn't winning every time. A lot of different factors go
into every race, and you can't control all of them. Success
means doing as excellent a job as you can on that particular
day. The people I admire most aren't necessarily the most
wonderful athletes. I admire the ones who keep coming back
and doing it, time after time."*
- AIMEE MULLINS, DOUBLE-AMPUTEE TRACK STAR

It is not easy to achieve success. And it is not easy to win the
game of chess. If it were easy everyone would achieve success
and win the game of chess, and their success would lose their
relevance. It requires immense attention, intelligence, focus and
strategy to win the game of chess. It requires lots of hard work,
smart work and wise work to achieve success. But both need
one common thing – that is strategy. Both need certain tools
and techniques. Hence, we will discuss them here.

When you want to win the game of chess you look at various
moves. You look at various permutations and combinations and
think several steps ahead of it. You also think ahead of the pros
and cons before making any move and anticipate the counter
moves by your opponent. In fact, chess is a brain game that
enhances your intelligence, focus, and decision-making.

Similarly, when you want to achieve success you need to look from multiple perspectives by setting short-term and long-term goals. First of all, you must be clear about your goals before you create a blueprint to reach your goals. While creating the blueprint you must keep both short-term and long-term goals in view and align them effectively to accomplish your goals. The reason for dividing goals into short-term and long-term is that if people fail to accomplish their short-term goals they are still motivated to move forward as they are focused on long-term goals.

Follow SMART Strategy

You must follow SMART strategy to accomplish your goals where SMART is the acronym for Specific, Measurable, Achievable, Realistic and Trackable. When you set your goals, be clear in what area of your life you want to excel. You must be able to measure how long it would take to accomplish your goals. You must see that the goals are achievable and realistic, and not based on daydreaming. Finally, you must be able to track the status of your goals from time to time so that you can take remedial action to accomplish your goals if you find distractions that are impeding your progress.

Although we want to reach our destination we must not forget to enjoy the journey as every moment of our life is precious. To conclude, achieving success in life is like playing the game of chess, and you must plan properly and execute effectively by making each move carefully to come out with flying colors.

"Winning doesn't always mean being first. Winning means you're doing better than you've ever done before."

— BONNIE BLAIR, OLYMPIC GOLD MEDALIST IN SPEED SKATING

CHAPTER 6

3 Aspects to Achieve Success

*"Unless you can subject your decision making to a ruthless and
continuous judgment by results, all your zigs and zags will
only be random lunges in the dark."*
- JAMES CHAMPY

To solve several problems, you need to consider various aspects but I have shortlisted the three key aspects - *confidence*, *information*, and *presence of mind*. Confidence is essential everywhere and in all areas but it is required more in problem-solving. Unless you are confident about the problem you will not be able to solve it. Secondly, you need to acquire information about the problem from all sources. Nowadays, information is the key to success. William Pollard once said, "Information is a source of learning. But unless it is organized, processed, and available to the right people in a format for decision making, it is a burden, not a benefit." Hence, acquire right and relevant information that will help you weigh all options to make a right decision. It requires your judgment and understanding the pros and cons of the fall-out. Thirdly, you must have presence of mind. There are people who are very knowledgeable but don't know how to handle as per the situation leading to failures. Having presence of mind tips the scale to your success. Hence, you must understand the ground realities and act accordingly to achieve the desired outcomes. To conclude, being confident, equipped with adequate information, and acting with 'presence of mind' not only solve the problems in your life but also lead to your success.

> *"Discovery of a solution consists of looking at the same thing as everyone else and thinking something different."*
>
> - ALBERT SZENT-GYORGYI

CHAPTER 7

Understand Id, Ego and Super Ego

*"The mind is its own place, and in itself can make a heaven of
Hell, a hell of Heaven."*
- JOHN MILTON

Sigmund Freud came up with several ideas and insights on psychology during his lifetime. Of which Id, Ego and Super Ego are very prominent. Id is an instinctive, irrational and imaginative one at the core of human mind with animal traits. Id can be compared with a demon. Ego is rational one that decides what is right and wrong and negotiates with Id and slows down Id's irrational ideas. Ego can be compared with a human being. Super Ego emphasizes on ethical and moral values and pursues great things and practices great values to stand out. Super Ego can be compared with an angel. Hence, the human mind is trifurcated into three compartments - Id, Ego and Super Ego where Id, Ego and Super Ego are synonymous with demon, human and angel respectively. Let us illustrate them with some examples here:

When a man finds a beautiful woman he wants to have sex with her by any means due to the influence of Id. Then Ego intervenes and advises not to think irrationally and act instinctively. It implores to talk to the woman for her consent and weigh the pros and cons before having sex thus acting rationally. Super Ego intervenes, and advises to love her, get her consent, and marry her to have sex regularly to enjoy a pleasant life thus emphasizing on moral and ethical values.

Here is another example where a man wants to become a millionaire by any means under the influence of Id. Then Ego enters and advises him to be rational and adopt right means and methods to become a millionaire. There is shift in human mind from irrational to rational. Finally, Super Ego intervenes to emphasize on ethical values in order to achieve the goal to become a millionaire. Hence, there is a constant battle between Id, Ego and Super Ego leading to conflicts within the mind which is known as intrapersonal conflict.

To conclude, crush your instinctive and irrational ideas and replace with rational and ethical values to excel as a fine human being and role model for others. Remember, no man is entirely good and no man is entirely bad as there are some positive aspects in every negative person and some negative aspects in every positive person. Understand Id, Ego and Super Ego and appreciate the realities to grow as a great person.

> *"The mind is a wonderful servant, but a terrible master."*
>
> – ROBIN SHARMA

CHAPTER 8

Set Your Goals

*"A dream is just a dream. A goal is a dream with a
plan and a deadline."*
- HARVEY MACKAY

We must set our goals in such a way that we will do things in a different manner to accomplish and achieve the impossible. When we do routine things routinely we get routine results. In contrast, when we do things differently we will achieve unique results. Hence, hereafter let us change the way we think, do and act to make our future better.

If you want to become a successful professional in your area of interest you must invest 1,000 hours regularly. It helps you establish and build your professional brand. Malcolm Gladwell, the Author of *Outliers* rightly said, "People who thrive put in at least 1000 hours of sustained, consistent training to reach their potential." Hence, choose your passionate area and then invest your precious time, energy and resources into it for 1,000 hours and I am sure you will be an expert in your domain and an authority in it. People look to you for your guidance and advice and you grow as a leader.

Remember that if you invest for 10,000 hours in your passionate area (3 years approximately) consistently, you become a regional celebrity. If you invest 20,000 hours (6 years approximately) you become a national celebrity. If you invest for 30,000 hours (9 years approximately) consistently you become an international celebrity.

Set SMART goals. Ensure that you ink your goals and read daily twice: after you get up from bed and before you go to bed. Divide your goals into short-term and long-term and align them without any contradiction. Keep moving forward by taking feedback regularly. One day you will find yourself on the top of the world where everyone looks to you for your guidance and you enjoy great respect.

> *"If you want to reach a goal, you must 'see the reaching' in your own mind before you actually arrive at your goal."*
>
> - ZIG ZIGLAR

CHAPTER 9

Spot Your Talents and Build Skills around them

*"The winners in life think constantly in terms of I can, I will,
and I am. Losers, on the other hand, concentrate their waking
thoughts on what they should have or would have done,
or what they can't do."*
– DENNIS WAITLEY

People often search for stones by leaving gems at home. There are a number of people who build skills by spending their money, energy and time by ignoring their inherent talents. They put the cart before the horse. In fact, they must first spot their hidden talents through psychometric instruments or by discussing with their parents. After discovering their talents they must choose the ones which are close to their hearts and pursue them based on the available resources, and then they must build skills and abilities around their talents. This process must go on regularly in the chosen domain to become an expert and achieve success consistently. They must also learn, unlearn and relearn to stay relevant and stand out.

Your strength consists of your inborn talents and gifts acquired from your parents, the kind of education and experience you have; and the skills, knowledge and abilities you have apart from other unique strengths that stand you out. Hence, spot your talents and unique strengths and capitalize them to achieve success. There are many people who don't know their strengths and leave this world without any contribution and achievement. Therefore, when you want to achieve something great you must learn to spot and tap your strengths and channel them effectively.

> *"Concentration of effort and the habit of working with a definite chief aim are two of the essential factors in success which are always found together. One leads to the other."*
>
> - NAPOLEON HILL

CHAPTER 10

The Skills the Employers Look for in Freshers

"All of the top achievers I know are life-long learners... Looking for new skills, insights, and ideas. If they're not learning, they're not growing...not moving toward excellence."
- DENIS WAITLEY

Employers are looking for certain skills in the freshers. Since many graduates are unemployed in India and the competition is fierce, there is more emphasis on other skills. Hence, the employers have become very particular in picking up the right candidates. The job aspirants must take immense interest to acquire skills and abilities apart from their academic knowledge and demonstrate the same during interview to grab employment offers.

Basic skills the employers look for among the freshers are self-management skills, job related skills, and transferable skills. The skills the organizations look for in the workplace are soft skills, hard skills and conceptual skills at all levels of management. Hence, the candidates must possess various skills which can be listed as succinctly as follows:

Attitude, confidence, communication skills, team building skills, negotiation skills, problem solving skills, leadership skills, decision-making, self-motivation, flexibility, adaptability, learning ability, computer literacy, good speaking, listening writing and reading skills; risk taking and ability to explore and experiment. Some of these qualities have been outlined by Stephen R. Covey in his book, *The 7 Habits of Highly Effective People*.

The candidates must outline these skills in their resumes and present them during interview to HR recruiters to create connectivity and enhance their employment prospects. In fact, the candidates must be careful during the first two minutes of the interview as it either makes or mars their job prospects. If the candidates are able to present what they outlined in their resumes they will have better prospects of grabbing the employment opportunities.

These skills vary from industry to industry and company to company. Hence, the candidates must do research about the company before going for an interview and must showcase their skills accordingly to enhance their employment prospects.

Presently the employers prefer offering the employment to the candidates who are employable and deployable; and are productive on the very first day. They look for plug and play candidates to minimize their costs they spend by way of training the freshers. Hence, candidates and especially freshers must do research before going for interview to come out with flying colors.

"Take advantage of every opportunity to practice your communication skills so that when important occasions arise, you will have the gift, the style, the sharpness, the clarity, and the emotions to affect other people."

- JIM ROHN

CHAPTER 11

Attitude is Your Asset

"Everything can be taken from a man but ... the last of the human freedoms - to choose one's attitude in any given set of circumstances, to choose one's own way."
- VICTOR FRANKL

In one of my soft skills training programs for freshers I taught various aspects of campus recruitment training including facing the employment interview. When I came out of the seminar hall a student asked me, "What is the meaning and definition of attitude?" I was excited to see his curiosity to learn about attitude. I explained attitude as follows:

Attitude is all about how you act rather than react to a situation. It is about how you procent and behave with others. It is about how you view the situation and the people around you.

Although the righteous man falls ten times he rises, but the wicked man never falls twice. If a person with a righteous attitude and values fails and falls God handholds and finally, he succeeds in his life. However, the wicked man with rotten attitude doesn't get another opportunity. Hence, attitude is an imperative to lead a happy and successful life. You must have a positive, right and strong attitude. Positive attitude means looking at the individuals, issues and ideas positively. Right attitude means adopting the right means and methods to accomplish your goals. And strong attitude means following your goals despite facing several challenges on your way to success. Precisely, attitude is your asset, and it keeps you firmly on your feet.

Build Your Attitude

> *"Our attitudes control our lives. Attitudes are a secret power working twenty-four hours a day, for good or bad. It is of paramount importance that we know how to harness and control this great force."*
>
> – BLAND TOM

The former Southwest Airlines CEO, Herb Kelleher once remarked, "We can change skill levels through training, but we can't change attitude." It is not correct. In fact, attitude can be changed the way skills can be honed. To some extent, changing the aptitude or upgrading the aptitude levels of the individuals is a more challenging task. However, changing the attitude, and building the attitude is an easier task as people change with the changing times. William James rightly remarked, "The greatest discovery of my generation is that human beings can alter their lives by altering their attitudes of mind."

When we look at both talents and skills, talents are inborn as individuals acquire by birth while skills can be acquired over a period of time including observation, learning, and experience. Here attitude is the way people perceive the situation or the people around them. It can be changed through teaching and training. When people set their goals they focus on their goals thus removing the negative thoughts they have. Research reveals that people get 60,000 thoughts on an average in a day and mostly they get negative thoughts. When they set goals they can remove the negative thoughts and replace with positive thoughts. In addition, there are a number of merits with goal setting. People stay focused as they set their goals. They will be able to mange their time effectively by weeding out the time wasting activities as they have set goals for themselves. They can enhance their longevity and above all, they can provide meaning to their lives. Hence, setting goals is one of the means of changing one's attitude and building a positive attitude.

There are several companies that emphasize on attitude while recruiting its talent. Google, Apple, Southwest, and The Four Seasons are some of the global companies that fall in this category. They believe in the slogan, *'hire for attitude and train for skills'*. Hence, the job aspirants must understand this fact and build positive, right and strong attitude to grab the employment opportunities, and to succeed in their professional lives.

> *"The block of granite which was an obstacle in the pathway of the weak, became a stepping-stone in the pathway of the strong."*
>
> — Thomas Carlyle

CHAPTER 12

Acquire Aptitude

*"I would say that IQ is the strongest predictor of which field
you can get into and hold a job in, whether you can be an
accountant, lawyer or nurse, for example."*
- DANIEL GOLEMAN

I conducted a soft skills training program for freshers recently. After completion of the session a student came along with me and asked, "Sir! Can you acquire aptitude?" I said, "Partly 'yes' and partly 'no'". There are different schools of thought about this. Aptitude is something people acquire through heredity. However, people can acquire if they are very serious about it.

People often confuse between attitude and aptitude. Attitude is about how you behave, and act to the situation. It is a psychological response to a situation, and how you view the things around you. In contrast, aptitude is about your mental abilities and flair for executing certain tasks. Attitude determines your altitude and you can cultivate attitude while aptitude helps you execute certain tasks effectively as you enjoy doing them.

Aptitude is about mental faculties and can be associated with talents. Talents are inborn while skills can be cultivated over a period of time. Those who want to join in Indian Air Force, they must qualify in Pilot Aptitude Battery Test (PABT). If a candidate is rejected s/he will not get another opportunity to take the test again as the recruiters believe that this aptitude cannot be cultivated. Similarly, most of the companies conduct aptitude tests to find out the aptitude levels of the job aspirants. Here if the candidates don't possess requisite aptitude levels they can practice and improve their aptitude levels. Hence, there are different schools of thoughts where some believe that people have it from heredity while some believe that people can acquire it through practice.

Remember that a right combination of attitude and aptitude will take you to success. You can associate EQ with attitude and IQ with aptitude. Hence, you must blend them proportionately to achieve your success.

"It is very important to understand that emotional intelligence is not the opposite of intelligence, it is not the triumph of heart over head - it is the unique intersection of both."

DAVID CARUSO, FROM "EMOTIONAL WHAT?"

CHAPTER 13

Be Effective to Achieve Greatness

"Whatever your present situation, I assure you that you are not your habits. You can replace old patterns of self-defeating behavior with new patterns, new habits of the effectiveness, happiness, and trust-based relationships."
- STEPHEN COVEY

I conducted a training program for students to equip them with some habits so that they can excel as successful professionals. I chose Stephen R. Covey's book, *7 Habits of Highly Effective People* and shared the seven habits outlined in it. Here are the habits:

1. Be Proactive
2. Begin with the End in Mind.
3. Put First Things First.
4. Think Win/Win.
5. Seek First to Understand, then to be Understood.
6. Synergize.
7. Sharpen the Saw

Subsequently I shared the 8th Habit from his book titled, *The 8th Habit From Effectiveness to Greatness*. Some of the students did not understand the meaning of effectiveness. Some responded that effectiveness is to work properly with good results, and some said that it is about perfection. I explained that effectiveness is about working in a smart way rather than a hard way in this competitive world to stand out from others. It is about executing the tasks with proper preparation and planning to achieve the desired outcomes within the stipulated time.

Effective people keep the end in mind, and take a little longer time in preparation and planning and execute the tasks within the stipulated time. They achieve multiple objectives within a short span. Hence, effectiveness is doing right things rather than things right. When you do things right it is known as efficiency, and when you do right things it is known as effectiveness. Efficiency is often associated with managers and effectiveness with leaders. To excel as a successful leader, you must be effective in your approach to achieve the organizational objectives. Here goes the story of Ram and Shyam following hard and smart work respectively:

A Story of Ram and Shyam

> *"If I had eight hours to chop down a tree, I'd spend six hours sharpening my axe."*
>
> — ABRAHAM LINCOLN

Ram and Shyam were given axes and asked to chop the tree within a span of one hour. Ram being the hard worker took the axe immediately and started to hit at the trunk of the tree. In contrast, Shyam took the axe and sharpened the axe for 15 minutes, and then chopped the tree within the span of 15 minutes. That means Shyam chopped the tree in 30 minutes. However, Ram took one hour and chopped the tree by struggling hard. When you look at them they did the work well in time but Ram did hard work while Shyam did smart work. Succinctly, Ram was efficient while Shyam was effective.

From this story, it is obvious that you have to be effective in order to accomplish your goals quickly. There are many people who do hard work but don't do smart work, thus lagging behind in their lives. This is a competitive world where most of the people work hard, and they are equipped with knowledge due to the access to internet and technology. But the people who think unconventionally and do smart work can grow rapidly.

When you look at some trainers they make a lot of fun in their training programs and the participants immensely enjoy the session. But at the end of the training there will not be any takeaways for the participants. However, when you look at a few trainers, you find that they nail hard the essence and bring out the behavioral changes among the participants. Such trainers command more respect as they impact and influence the minds of the participants deeply. Remember that an hour of effective teaching is better than years of teaching that doesn't ensure takeaways among the audiences.

Whenever you want to do any work you must learn to put in your best efforts keeping multiple outcomes in view. In this way, you can save your time and reach your goals quickly in your life.

To conclude, do smart work, qualitative work, and be effective to achieve greatness in your life.

> *"Efficiency is doing things right; effectiveness is doing the right things."*
>
> — PETER F. DRUCKER

CHAPTER 14

Be an Example to Excel as a Leader

"Effective leadership starts with Example and ends with Ethics and imbedded throughout this process are the factors of Energy, Enthusiasm, Endurance, Emotional Intelligence, Eloquence, Empowerment, Effectiveness, Execution, and Excellence. All are necessary to excel as a successful leader. Any shortcoming or deficiency in any one of these elements inevitably creates an imbalance in leadership effectiveness."
- PROFESSOR M.S.RAO

Leaders like Mahatma Gandhi, Martin Luther King Jr. and Mother Teresa are examples of successful leaders. Ordinary individuals take them as their role models; ape them; and aspire to grow like them because these leaders raised their bars and grew in stature by serving others and setting an example for others to follow. They are legends beyond their lifetimes. They are successful leaders because they never craved for success. They always gave their best to others through their selfless services and sacrifices. Do you also want to become an exemplary leader like them? Let us discuss exemplary leadership in this regard.

What is Exemplary Leadership?

Do you lead by words or deeds? If you lead only by words, you will be called a rhetoric leader. If you lead only by deeds, you will be called a performing leader. If you lead by words and deeds where there is no gap between preaching and practice, you will be called an exemplary leader. Exemplary leadership calls for walking your talk and setting an example for others to follow. Albert Schweitzer rightly said, "Example is not the main thing in influencing others, it is the only thing." It is the example that works wonders rather than anything else to influence and impact your followers. And when you set an example for others you will achieve the desired outcomes and success.

Is Leadership Synonymous with Success?

Success is the sweetest word for everyone. Everyone craves for success but only a few achieve it. And those who achieve it are known as leaders in the society. In fact, leadership is different from success. Leaders work to achieve their desired goals and objectives. Once they accomplish their objectives they are known as successful people. In reality, success is a by-product for leaders, not an end-product. Additionally, we often take leaders as examples of success. In fact, leaders undergo tons of trials and tribulations, encounter failures and accept brickbats to finally receive bouquets of success. Hence, success doesn't come easily to others as it involves lots of struggles, sacrifices and risk-taking. Leaders undertake their journey when there seems to be no light at the end of the tunnel for their followers. But leaders know where they are going and why they are going as they are visionaries with convictions and lead through confidence and optimism.

If you want to achieve success like leaders be mentally prepared to contribute your best without expecting any rewards from others. Have a vision. Influence others. Motivate your followers. Align their energies and efforts as per your desired objectives and goals. And finally, accomplish your objectives to soar like an eagle.

> *"I think leadership comes from integrity – that you do whatever you ask others to do. I think there are non-obvious ways to lead. Just by providing a good example as a parent, a friend, a neighbor makes it possible for other people to see better ways to do things. Leadership does not need to be a dramatic, fist in the air and trumpets blaring activity."*
>
> - SCOTT BERKUN

CHAPTER 15

Manage External Threats to Excel as a Leader

"There comes a special moment in everyone's life, a moment for which that person was born. That special opportunity, when he seizes it, will fulfill his mission — a mission for which he is uniquely qualified. In that moment he finds greatness.
It is his finest hour."
- WINSTON CHURCHILL

Why do some people succeed while some people fail in their lives? It is the persistence that makes all the difference! Those who persist despite facing failures will succeed finally, and those who give up will not be able to achieve success.

There are two things you must manage in your life — internal and external factors. Internal factors are within your control while the external factors are beyond your control. Most of the people take precautions and avoid internal challenges through preparation and anticipation. However, people cannot anticipate external challenges. When faced with external challenges most of the people often get vexed and give up ultimately. Here comes the difference between the followers and the leaders.

The followers give up and follow others while the leaders persist and face the challenges head-on, and address effectively by finding out the root causes thus managing the challenges successfully. The leaders ensure that things don't go out of their control. However, when they find that the things are going out of control, they apply their complete mental faculties, and put entire efforts to ensure that the things are falling in line as per their expectations. Remember that those who succeed in managing external threats by putting things on the track through persistence will succeed ultimately. Hence, you must learn to address the issues and put the things on the main track from time to time to soar like a leader.

"Luck is what happens when preparation meets opportunity."
\- ELMER LETTERMAN

CHAPTER 16

Participate in JAM Sessions

"I only wish I could find an institute that teaches people how to listen. Business people need to listen at least as much as they need to talk. Too many people fail to realize that real communication goes in both directions."
- LEE IACOCCA, FORMER CEO, CHRYSLER CORPORATION

JAM is the acronym for *Just A Minute.* In this session, students are asked to speak on a topic of their choice or on a given topic for a minute. It is conducted for students to improve their communication skills and build confidence. It helps the introvert and shy students take initiative and speak on the topic for a minute. It helps students condense the entire essence precisely in their mind, and speak only the relevant aspects within a minute. In addition, it can be used during the teaching session as well by the teachers. After completion of the teaching session, the teachers can ask the volunteers or handpick some students and ask them to speak what they understood about the session. By this, students will be able to listen and learn well. It is an integral part of *Meka's Method,* an innovative teaching tool coined by this author.

Some companies conduct JAM sessions during their employment interview to test the communication skills of the candidates. That is the reason JAM is included in Campus Recruitment Training Programs to encourage students to improve their communication skills enhance their employability skills. Hence, students must actively participate in JAM sessions in educational institutions to improve their communication skills and grab employment opportunities.

> *"The two words 'information' and 'communication' are often used interchangeably, but they signify quite different things. Information is giving out; communication is getting through."*
>
> - SYDNEY J. HARRIS

CHAPTER 17

Blend Hard and Soft Skills

"In today's competitive environment, it is not enough to be the best in your field, intellectually. Competency is only half of what you need to climb the ladder of success. The other half is the softer side of you – it's that part of you that will be liked, admired, trusted and remembered."
– CAROLE NICOLA IDES

Why do some film stars succeed while some fade away? At times film stars with a little talent enter into the film industry, have a foothold and hang on to it for a longer time. On the other hand, there are film stars who have a huge potential but fail to survive in the industry. It is basically because film stars must learn to blend hard and soft skills. In this connection, let us know the difference between the hard and the soft skills. Hard skills are about technical competence while soft skills are about polite and pleasing way of communicating with others. In the case of film stars, hard skills are about their acting skills and talent while soft skills are about their ability to get along with other stars and other stakeholders including directors, and producers.

Soft skills is defined as the skills and abilities related to your personality, attitude and behavior. At times people who are good at hard skills develop high ego and gradually lose their base. In fact, it is vital to mix both hard and soft skills judiciously to achieve professional success. At the same time, the film stars can survive only when they can successfully blend their Intelligence Quotient (IQ) with Emotional Quotient (EQ). IQ is something people are blessed with through heredity while EQ can be cultivated over a period of time. In fact, it is the EQ which is crucial for the success of people rather than IQ as the individuals with high IQ come with their egos and fail in the corporate world.

Although there are a number of factors that are responsible for the success of the stars in the film industry such as network, placing and timing, it is the right application of soft skills that will take them towards success quickly. Therefore, people must learn to blend their soft and hard skills, and EQ and IQ proportionately to achieve career success and ensure professional longevity. Do remember the slogan: people rise in the industry due to hard skills and fall flat due to dearth of soft skills.

> *"Communication is a skill that you can learn. It's like riding a bicycle or typing. If you're willing to work at it, you can rapidly improve the quality of very part of your life."*
>
> *- BRIAN TRACY*

CHAPTER 18

Acquire Smart Skills to Stand out as a Smart Leader

"A smart man makes a mistake, learns from it, and never makes that mistake again. But a wise man finds a smart man and learns from him how to avoid the mistake altogether."
- ROY H. WILLIAMS

In one of my soft skills training programs I explained about soft and hard skills to my participants where soft skills are the way one communicates with others in a pleasing and polite manner and hard skills are the technical skills, domain competency and the knowledge one possesses. All professionals need soft and hard skills to succeed at the workplace. One of the participants asked me what we should call when we mix both hard and soft skills. I found the question quite interesting. I replied to him that the proportional and judicious mix of hard and soft skills is known as smart skills.

Smart skills are the blend of hard and soft power, hard and soft skills, technical and business acumen. Flexibility and adaptability are the key components of smart skills. Therefore, we can define smart leadership as the process of setting goals, influencing people, building effective teams, motivating people, and, finally, aligning their energies and efforts towards organizational goals and objectives through soft and hard skills; soft and hard power and technical and business acumen.

The smart leaders are situational leaders who adopt transactional and transformational leadership; blend both efficiency and effectiveness; believe in hard and smart work; and do right things. Leaders like Jeff Immelt of General Electric, Michael Dell of Dell Computers, and Steve Jobs of Apple Computers fall in the category of smart leadership. Hence, smart leaders are essential to walk the talk to achieve the desired outcomes successfully by blending both people-orientation and task-orientation.

Currently Gen Y appreciates working in flat organizations and in collegial model of behavior where they don't want to work under demanding bosses and commanding superiors, but prefer to work with the leaders who can handhold and guide them at the workplace. Hence, being good at smart skills helps immensely at the workplace for superiors and subordinates, and adopting smart leadership helps greatly for the leaders to get the tasks executed effectively in order to accomplish the organizational goals and objectives. To conclude, acquire smart skills to stand out as a smart leader.

> *"Leadership is the ability to establish standards and manage a creative climate where people are self-motivated toward the mastery of long term constructive goals, in a participatory environment of mutual respect, compatible with personal values."*
>
> — MIKE VANCE

CHAPTER 19

Possess Inquisitiveness

"A teacher is a compass that activates the magnets of curiosity, knowledge, and wisdom in the pupils."
- TERRI GUILLEMETS

When I asked my elder son, M. Ganesh Sai the name of his principal, he replied that he did not know. I told him, "You must know the name of your principal as he is the head of your educational institution and also you must know the name of the president of our country."   I further added that these are the basic things students must be aware of. He further added that most of his friends were not aware of the principal's name. I advised him that basic information such as name of the principal and the president of the country is a must for everyone to know. For instance, when you go for an employment interview the recruiter may ask couple of questions about the noted personalities in your country to test whether you are aware of basic information and also to test your inquisitiveness. If you express your ignorance it conveys wrong impression on the mind of the recruiters. My son asked me to explain about inquisitiveness. I explained to him about inquisitiveness as follows:

Inquisitiveness is about being curious about various things that happen around you. It is the catalyst for motivation. It is essential in the present world. Inquisitiveness helps you ask right questions and learn various things. It helps you acquire knowledge quickly and also retain it for a longer time. Therefore, inquisitiveness helps you stand out from others. It helps you invent new things leading to innovation. In the current cut-throat competitive world, the people who have extra essential information have an edge over others. Information is the key to survival and success. When you have adequate information you will be able to understand well, and be able to make sound decisions and achieve success ultimately.

Students must possess inquisitiveness to learn various aspects in life. We often think that inquisitiveness is needed only in classrooms but it is needed beyond classrooms. Therefore, equip yourself with inquisitiveness and acquire more essential information in your area of interest to stand out.

> *"Effective questioning brings insight, which fuels curiosity, which cultivates wisdom."*
>
> – CHIP BELL

CHAPTER 20

Learn Effectively

"You can teach a student a lesson for a day; but if you can teach him to learn by creating curiosity, he will continue the learning process as long as he lives."
- CLAY P. BEDFORD

Indian students are smart in memorizing the content and reproducing it effectively during the examinations and making grades. Does it pay in the long run?

Indian education encourages 3Rs – read, write and reproduce. Most of the students work hard to cram the content without knowing its implications and applications. In addition, teachers encourage students by giving them a lot of notes rather than encourage them to think critically and conceptually.

According to Sylvia Downs and Patricia Perry, there are three ways of learning. First is learning by memorizing which enables the individuals to recall material in the same form as it was originally learned. Secondly, learning by understanding where understanding is an active mental process involving thoughts which link or group ideas in a new way that makes sense to the individual. Thirdly, learning by doing which involves learning a procedure and then practicing it until the individual becomes skilful. These three methods of learning can be called MUD which is the acronym for memorizing, understanding, and doing. When we look at Indian education from the perspective of MUD, it mostly emphasizes on memorizing, neglecting the other two areas – understanding and doing. Hence, Indian educators and students must equally focus on understanding the key concepts and exploring things through practice to learn effectively. They must think critically, analyze logically, and apply effectively to achieve the desired outcomes out of Indian education. When the learners understand the concepts properly they can apply in innumerable areas and reap rewards out of them. Remember the sage words of James Truslow Adams: "There are obviously two educations. One should teach us how to make a living and the other how to live."

> *"Learning is an active process. We learn by doing. Only knowledge that is used sticks in your mind."*
>
> — DALE CARNEGIE

Reference
Alan Mumford: Effective Learning

CHAPTER 21

Read Your Manuscript Aloud

"There are always three speeches, for every one you actually gave. The one you practiced, the one you gave, and the one you wish you gave."
- DALE CARNEGIE

I was invited to lead a webinar on "Soft Leadership" by International Leadership Association in 2012. To make the webinar successful, the organizer invited me for practice webinar twice. I wrote key ideas and insights about the concept, and made it into a synopsis, and I started to read it aloud for preparation for the practice webinar. I was amazed to find a lot of improvement within me as I created more ideas and insights, improved my accent, and realized the grammatical mistakes that I make. I decided to apply this idea whenever I send manuscripts for publication to prestigious global journals. In fact, there are several advantages when you read aloud. Here are a few of them:

- When you read aloud, you hear your own voice and find out if there are any inaccuracies while presenting your content.

In contrast, when you read within yourself, you don't hear, and often don't observe any inaccuracies.

- When you read aloud, you will be able to hear your voice and observe the areas where you need to improve your accent. By focusing on those areas where you find it difficult to pronounce, you will be able to substitute with the words that are easy for you to pronounce. This is applicable when you deliver presentation for a gathering. Over a period of time, you will be able to minimize variations from the accepted standards of your accent, and neutralize your accent and become a successful speaker.

- It is said, 'to teach is to learn twice' because while teaching you develop more clarity, improve your communication skills, and thought process. However, you cannot jot down the points during the teaching session. When you read your script aloud during non-teaching sessions, you may jot down the ideas you get immediately as you can stop reading the script aloud for some in order to write down the main ideas.

Finally, I read the manuscript aloud seven times, improved the script, and successfully led the webinar. Hence, don't be ashamed to read your manuscript aloud when you want to impact your audience and ensure effective takeaways to them. Joseph Addison rightly said, "Reading is to the mind what exercise is to the body." Great speakers like Winston Churchill and Abraham Lincoln did a lot of practice before they delivered their speeches, and excelled as great orators.

"To read is to fly: it is to soar to a point of vantage which gives a view over wide terrains of history, human variety, ideas, shared experience and the fruits of many inquiries."

— A C GRAYLING, FINANCIAL TIMES

CHAPTER 22

Manage Your Time

*"If the creator had a purpose in equipping us with a neck, he
surely meant us to stick it out."*
- ARTHUR KOESTLER

I play three roles in a day. I get up early in the morning as I am
an early riser. I author books in the area of leadership
development. I make use of my best potential and uncork my
hidden talents and explore various things as my body supports
it. My mind is my boss and does whatever the good it can do for
others. My mind goes all over the world covering on various
aspects and expressing my dreams and passion. Subsequently
I keep reading the best content in my passionate area of
leadership development. I read quality books and browse
qualitative blogs and read the content written by international
leadership experts who present different perspectives. I read
and generate more ideas thus adding value to my existing
knowledge base. In fact, I enjoy reading, and appreciate
learning continuously to add value to my knowledge. While
reading I get new triggers and find out what is missing and
address the same. I explore how to fill those existing gaps.
Subsequently I eliminate irrelevant ideas and negative

individuals who I meet and do not add any value to my knowledge base and to my life. Before I go to my bed I empty my mind from information overload and also individuals' overload, and plan for the next day and fall asleep. This is how I do every day. Precisely, I am the creator in the morning as I write books; I am the generator in the afternoon as I keep learning new things, acquire new ideas and insights and create new triggers; and I am the destroyer in the night as I eliminate irrelevant individuals and outdated knowledge from my mind. To put it in the Hindu philosophy, I am the Lord Brahma in the morning; I am the Lord Vishnu in the afternoon; and I am the Lord Shiva in the night. I play these three roles everyday and will continue to play for the rest of my life.

Remember that God gifted 24 hours to everyone. Hence, you must learn to make use of your time in such a way that you enjoy the journey of your life and reach your destination of success through effective time management.

> *"Time has a way of getting away from us, because we never have a grip on it during the day..."*
>
> - DOUG FIREBAUGH

CHAPTER 23

Employment is not an Affair between the Employees and Employers

"When I interview somebody, I look at their resume to see what they've done, who they've worked with, and how many times. If they've gotten repeat work, those are the kinds of actors I want to hire."
- JOE PANTOLIANO

I conducted soft skills training program for students on the topic 'Facing the interview board'. During mock-interview session, a student responded to my question - "Why should I hire you?" as follows: "I would be loyal and work very long years in your organization." I probed her how long? She replied that she would work forever. I replied that nowadays employment has become an affair between the employees and the employers. Previously employment was considered a marriage, and it was treated as a lifelong commitment to the organization. In fact, the Japanese management emphasizes on lifelong commitment to organizations wherein the employees' commitment to organizations is like a marriage. In contrast, the western management treats it as an affair because the employers retain the employees as long as they perform well. According to this system, if employees don't perform well they will be served with pink slips without any second thought. The Japanese management gives a number of opportunities to employees to upgrade themselves as it believes more in 'concern for people'. In the western management, it is more of 'task orientation' rather than 'people orientation'. We have another management system, Theory Z propounded by William Ouchi who blended the best of both the American management and the Japanese management.

Finally, I told the student to reply to the question as follows: You must project your self-management skills, transferable skills, and job related skills. Since you are a fresher, you must showcase more on your academic achievements and other extra-curricular achievements so that you will have better chances of landing the employment offer.

> *"A successful life is one that is lived through understanding and pursuing one's own path, not chasing after the dreams of others."*
>
> − CHIN-NING CHU

CHAPTER 24

Stay Away from Suicidal Tendencies

"God allows us to experience the low points of life in order to teach us lessons we could not learn in any other way. The way we learn those lessons is not to deny the feelings but to find the meanings underlying them."
- STANLEY LINDQUIST

It is unfortunate that suicides are increasing at an alarming rate in India and especially in South India with Andhra Pradesh topping in number of suicides. It is sad to note that people commit suicide on petty issues and especially Indian youth are committing more on insignificant issues. Research reveals that next to road accidents it is the suicides leading to loss of Indian youth. Most of the suicides could have been averted if the youth were counseled properly and guided timely.

Youth are often carried away by temporary emotions and cut short their lives. They must realize that God has given them life and He alone can take it. Some of the causes among the youth are due to failure in love, academic pressure, poor performance, unable to live up to parental expectations, and financial hardships.

Acquire Emotional Quotient (EQ)

Life is full of ups and downs and people must learn to balance their emotions and motivate their emotions especially when they hit lows in their lives. If they exercise restraint and hold positive thoughts for a few seconds they'll be able to bounce back from depression and stay motivated. When they are depressed and carried away by suicidal tendencies they must consult doctors or share their inner feelings with their family members or trusted friends to find comfort and come out with solutions. In this regard, people should understand emotional intelligence quotient (EQ) where it's a fivefold process of identifying their emotions, managing their emotions, motivating their emotions, identifying the emotions of others and managing them. When the affected people find themselves in depression mode they must learn to manage and motivate their emotions to bounce back to normalcy quickly.

Observe Children

It has been observed that the people who've suicidal tendencies demonstrate abnormal behaviour, different mood levels and often stay aloof from others. When parents find such tendencies in their children they must spend some time with their children to connect and create emotional stability. Parents should not exert any pressure on their children especially to score high grades and marks. It may result in feeling guilty or depressed when they don't perform well. Parents must encourage competitive and collaborative spirit among their children to enable them to compete and collaborate as per the situation. If children don't perform well academically they should be placed in their areas of interest or aptitude to enable them to enjoy what they like and grow in their lives. Parents must not compare their children with others as everyone is unique in this world with unique gifts and talents. In addition, when they compare their children with others they are insulting their children by downplaying their children's' unique strengths and talents. Parents must also monitor movements of their children and their friends with whom they move closely to understand their pulse and act accordingly.

Take Action

Here are a few steps to check suicidal tendencies and bounce back from depression:

- Set goals in your life. When you set goals you can remove your negative thoughts and replace them with positive thoughts. You can manage your time and stay focused clearly on your goals to provide meaning to your life.
- Think positive and be positive through your inner dialogue. We all have inner dialogue wherein we talk to ourselves throughout the day. Set a positive tone for the dialogue to become positive and behave positive.
- Surround yourself with positive people. When you are in the midst of positive people you get positive vibes and grow into a healthy individual.
- Hit gym regularly or do meditation or go for a walk as it builds high energy levels and provides you with a positive outlook towards life.
- Talk to someone with whom you feel comfortable when you hit lows.

- Take meals regularly to fuel your body constantly with energy and enthusiasm.
- Read good books, magazines and novels to acquire knowledge and build a positive attitude.
- Find out your passionate areas and pursue your hobbies. When you pursue them you enjoy your life fully and also build a network of likeminded friends.
- Have fun in life. Enjoy your present life without worrying about the unpleasant past and the unpredictable future.
- Consult psychiatrist when you hit lows frequently to get timely help.
- Enjoy your journey of life to reach your final destination of success.
- Above all, look at the door that is open, not the one that is closed.

Face Challenges Squarely

Suicide is not the solution for any problem in the world. If suicide is the only solution we will find only dead bodies on the earth as all human beings have problems. The truth is that some people reveal their problems while some conceal their problems as mindset of the people is different from one another.

It is rightly said, 'when God solves your problems, you have faith in his abilities….When He doesn't solve your problems, He has faith in your abilities…" Hence, face the challenges head-on. When the going gets tough, tough gets going. Life is incomplete without peaks and valleys. Remember that it is the weak who commit suicide while the strong survive in the world. Hence, be a strong person and face the battles in your life.

God has created you with some purpose. You have only one life. Your role is to execute your tasks effectively and leave this world a better place to live for others. Do your duties sincerely. Always think of contributing your best to make a difference in the lives of others. You've no right to take your life. No religion encourages suicide. Remember, it is a privilege to be born as a human being.

> *"Count your blessings. Once you realize how valuable you are and how much you have going for you, the smiles will return, the sun will break out, the music will play, and you will finally be able to move forward in the life that God intended for you with grace, strength, courage, and confidence."*
>
> - OG MANDINO

CHAPTER 25

Build Your Brand

*"Even individuals need to develop a brand for themselves ....
Whatever your area of expertise, you can take steps to make
people think of YOU when they think of your field."*
- ACCELEPOINT WEBZINE

Everyone craves for building their brand. But very few people are aware of the tools and techniques essential to build their brands. Here is a three-step process to build your brand:

1. Excel as an expert. To become an expert, focus on your passionate area. Find out your innate talents rather than focusing on skills. Talents are inborn which people acquire from their parents. People have talents by birth. They must spot their talents and tap them. Then they must focus clearly on their goals and build skills around their inborn talents. In this way, they can grow as experts.

2. Share your knowledge with others. You cannot reach out to entire audience physically. Hence, you must author books in your area of interest so that you can reach out to the world. You can also blog articles in your area.

3. Interact with people in your core area. When you interact with people they will pose questions about your domain knowledge. You can do research in those areas and improve your knowledge base. This interaction builds connections with others thus enhancing your visibility.

To summarize, focus on your talents and build skills around them; share your knowledge through your books; and interact with likeminded people to grow in your area of interest to build your brand.

> *"Branding demands commitment; commitment to continual re-invention; striking chords with people to stir their emotions; and commitment to imagination. It is easy to be cynical about such things, much harder to be successful."*
>
> - SIR RICHARD BRANSON, CEO, VIRGIN

CHAPTER 26

Build Your Fan Base

"True leadership must be for the benefit of the followers not the enrichment of the leaders."
- ROBERT TOWNSEND

When you look at celebrities they build a huge fan base who follow them and shield them as and when required. When celebrities are in crisis the fan base helps them greatly as fans stand by them. But creating an army of fan base is not an easy task. You must have domain expertise to create a set of selective followers. You must have principles and stick to them through thick and thin. You must care for and connect with your fans from time to time to keep them motivated. It requires your time, money, energy and resources to build an army of fan base.

Political, corporate, religious leaders, sportspersons, and film stars create their fan base that gives them great strength. It makes them more accountable and responsible. It provides meaning to their lives. Political leaders like Abraham Lincoln and Mahatma Gandhi live beyond their lifetimes due to their impeccable integrity, ethics and values.

When celebrities have poor health the fans pray for their good health. When they experience lows, their fan base keeps their survival intact. You can create your fan base through various means and ways including usage of social media, interacting with people in your area of interest and participating in NGO activities. Once you build your fan base you can convey your message to society and make a huge difference. Hence, build a huge army of fan base to stand out.

> *"A true Master is not the one with the most students, but one who creates the most Masters. A true leader is not the one with the most followers, but one who creates the most leaders."*
>
> — NEALE DONALD WALSCH

CHAPTER 27

Make Peace to Progress

*"Those who fight fire with fire burn their houses
down twice as fast."*
- VIETNAMESE PROVERB

Some people have the habit of fighting on trivial issues, and criticizing petty individuals thus losing pretty opportunities in their lives. They don't realize that a lot of energy is wasted by thinking about negative individuals. They often think about others and plan the ways and means to topple others. It is a retrograde step indeed! In fact, when you want to grow in your life, adopt the concept of 'forgive and forget' so that you find more time to concentrate on important activities thus providing meaning to your life. You will be elevated among others with your kind heart, and also you will make quick progress in your life.

We often find some countries fighting against each other on petty issues or on egoistic issues resulting in casualties of precious resources. At times, supremacy of a community may lead to declaring war thus wasting their precious resources. Such countries lose not only men, machine, money and material but they lose peace, and create problems for their own people. Hence, whether it is countries or individuals, it is essential to focus on positive things ignoring negative things in order to progress. To conclude, develop a mindset of 'forgive and forget' and focus on positive aspects to progress, and to make a difference in the lives of others.

> *"Realize that true happiness lies within you. Waste no time and effort searching for peace and contentment and joy in the world outside. Remember that there is no happiness in having or in getting, but only in giving. Reach out. Share. Smile. Hug. Happiness is a perfume you cannot pour on others without getting a few drops on yourself."*
>
> - OG MANDINO

CHAPTER 28

Education versus Experience

"Do you know the difference between education and experience? Education is when you read the fine print; experience is what you get when you don't."
- PETE SEEGER

People often debate the supremacy of education over experience, and vice versa. The topic generates lots of debate as there are different schools of thought. Let us look at the pros and cons of education and experience in this regard.

Education gives you knowledge, skills and abilities. It opens the door to the outside world. It builds in you tons of confidence to take on several challenges head-on. It also provides you with employment opportunities and you can earn your livelihood out of it. On the other hand, experience gives you confidence to handle tasks effectively apart from enhancing your intuition and gut feelings. There are people without elementary education who made it big in their lives due to their experience. But most of them regretted not having education. Some of them felt that they could have done better if they had acquired education.

Presently the working executives realized the importance of higher education, and are doing various courses to support their experience in order to scale the corporate ladder quickly. Since competition is stiff, the working executives find pursuing various courses is beneficial to ensure their quick career success.

When you look at college dropouts like Steve Jobs, Michael Dell, Bill Gates, and Mark Zuckerberg, it is clear that they are successful as entrepreneurs. At the same time, we cannot rush to conclusion that educated people don't succeed as entrepreneurs. Similarly, there are people who excelled without formal education. These people learned through the hard way, by trial and error method and learned bitter lessons in life and succeeded finally.

If education enhances Intelligence Quotient (IQ), experience enhances Emotional Quotient (EQ). You need to blend education and experience to excel as an effective leader. A rich experience without any education and a rich education without any experience creates imbalance among the individuals. Therefore, those who have good education must complement with experience and those who have great experience must complement with good education to achieve success in their lives. To sum up, right and judicious blend of education and experience will take you towards your quick career success.

> *"A mind that is stretched by a new experience can never go back to its old dimensions."*
>
> - OLIVER WENDELL HOLMES, JR.

CHAPTER 29

Education is not for Employment Alone

"Education is the best friend. An educated person is respected everywhere. Education beats the beauty and the youth."
\- CHANAKYA

Most Indians think that education is only for employment. They must understand that education is basically for empowerment and mostly for enlightenment. It provides you basic strength and support to survive in the world, and teaches you to learn lessons and succeed in your life. If you are educated, you become independent and you can do many things by yourself without depending much on others. It provides you basic confidence and you can survive in any part of the world. Education serves as a launching pad for your career and life. It opens the window to the outside world. It helps you stand firmly on your feet and handhold others. It helps you bring the change the way you want in others and society. When you pursue your passion and other areas other than for employment, and if there are any setbacks, you can take support of education and go for employment. Hence, education is not merely for employment but for empowerment. Education is beyond employment and above enlightenment. Remember the words of John F. Kennedy, "The goal of education is the advancement of knowledge and the dissemination of truth."

"Education will help you in adversity when your passion fails to take you to prosperity."

– PROFESSOR M.S.RAO

CHAPTER 30

Education is Incomplete without Extracurricular Activities

*"The extracurricular activity in which I was most engaged -
debating - helped shape my interests in public policy."*
- JOSEPH E STIGLITZ

Currently Indian educational institutions emphasize more on curricular activities rather than on extracurricular activities. In fact, education is complete only when curricular and extracurricular activities are accorded equally importance. Classroom education, especially curricular activities provide theoretical knowledge. Education empowers and enlightens students by opening window to the outside world. A person without education is considered to be blind. At the same time, students must also focus on extracurricular activities like playing games and sports, and organizing events which enhance emotional intelligence and promote camaraderie and fraternity. They also promote competitive spirit and help them understand team dynamics. As a result, students build leadership skills and abilities which are very much essential in today's world. Hence, it is imperative to blend curricular and extracurricular activities among students to enable them to blossom into successful personalities.

Recently I was invited to attend a college anniversary day. One of the students outlined the challenges and several stumbling blocks he encountered but finally bounced back to normalcy. I appreciated his sincerity for acknowledging publicly and his ability to bounce back with resilience and tenacity. I supported his views and enlightened the students that nobody can become a crackshot unless he loses some ammunition. Real leadership qualities can be learnt at the ground level, and especially through failing, falling and bouncing back. Hence, students must learn that things won't happen the way they want, but will happen the way they are supposed to happen as there are certain aspects in the external environment which are beyond human control. However, we can predict and prepare to some extent, and be able to manage external threats to execute the tasks effectively to accomplish our goals. To conclude, students must not only focus on their curricular activities, they must also emphasize on extracurricular activities as the curricular activities equip students with knowledge and the extracurricular activities equip them with skills and abilities. There is need for all students to possess knowledge, skills and abilities to succeed in the current competitive world.

> *"When I was a teenager, I began to settle into school because I'd discovered the extracurricular activities that interested me: music and theater."*
>
> – MORGAN FREEMAN

CHAPTER 31

S. Radhakrishnan – A True Academic Leader

"Teachers are true nation builders. A teacher or a 'Guru' is revered in our society for mentoring our children, building their character and preparing them to face larger challenges of life."
- S. RADHAKRISHNAN

Every year, Indians celebrate September 5th as Teacher's Day to commemorate the birth anniversary of S. Radhakrishnan. He is an amazing example of an academician reaching to the highest position of office - President of India. He showed to everyone that teachers are leaders, and can influence beyond their academic career through their deeds, which become examples worthy of emulation.

He was born in Tituttani in Tamilnadu to poor parents who initially thought of making him a priest. But his parents recognized his abilities early and encouraged him to pursue studies. He pursued his education through scholarships. He led Andhra University and Banaras Hindu University. His abilities and capabilities were spotted, and he was made as the Vice

President of India. Pundit Nehru spotted his abilities, and finally he was made as the President of India.

Being born as poor is neither a sin, nor a liability. The present youth should learn lessons from the biography of S. Radhakrishnan. They must emulate his values and principles and work hard to make India a prosperous country in the world. According to the Hindu philosophy, teacher has been accorded the third highest position next to mother and father. Hence, teachers must play a crucial role to live up to the expectations of students, to contribute their best and make a difference in the lives of their pupils.

"A teacher affects eternity; he can never tell where his influence stops."

- HENRY B ADAMS

Be a Responsible Educator

"It requires a lot of courage to become an educator as it is not for everybody. If a parent is unworthy, children are spoiled; if a doctor neglects his duty, the patient dies; if an engineer performs poorly, the infrastructure collapses; and if an educator makes a mistake, an entire generation is ruined."
– PROFESSOR M.S. RAO

Educators must play crucial role in shaping their students. They must treat teaching not only as a profession but also as a responsibility to infuse principles, values, and ethics among students, apart from sharing their knowledge. Although teaching is a profession they must go beyond their profession and work with passion to shape students into healthy personalities. If they are passionate and responsible they can influence more than parents in shaping the students as successful and worthy citizens.

Customize Your Teaching

While teaching, educators must reach out to all kinds of students with different teaching styles as per the students' learning levels. They must do research in their areas constantly and update their knowledge regularly. They must learn, unlearn and relearn constantly to stay updated.

Groom Well-rounded Personalities

Educators must regularly attend the classes and take the attendance of students; teach well; conduct tests periodically; assess them; provide them feedback for their improvement; encourage the areas in which students can grow constantly; and upgrade their skills and abilities. They must develop students holistically by encouraging curricular and extracurricular activities thus shaping them into well-rounded personalities. Succinctly, educators must think of adding value to students rather than adding value to themselves.

Walk Your Talk

Students learn mostly by example rather than by rhetoric. Hence, educators must walk their talk and motivate students regularly. They must not only teach but also observe the behavior of the students. They must build good attitude among the students and build personalities that are well-tuned to the established standards, principles and practices to lead their lives meaningfully.

Be a Responsible Educator

If you don't crave for making money but crave for shaping the personalities of students, teaching is the best profession. You can earn respect only if you can teach well. Remember that you cannot make money out of it but you can only command respect and derive great satisfaction. Hence, take all aspects into view before becoming an educator. Once you identify your passion for teaching, firm up your mind to become an educator, be responsible and accountable while adding value to students.

"In a completely rational society, the best of us would be teachers and the rest of us would have to settle for something less, because passing civilization along from one generation to the next ought to be the highest honor and the highest responsibility anyone could have."

\- LEE IACOCCA

CHAPTER 33

Be a Coach like Lord Shri Krishna

"No matter how strong a person mentally is, without proper mental nourishment he or she will crumble. Personal coaching is one of the best ways to help you get that nourishment and to keep you stay focused."
– BEINGLIVE.COM

In the Mahabharata epic, Lord Krishna can be compared with a great coach who coached Arjun when the latter was hitting lows after seeing the army of relatives against whom he had to fight in the battlefield of Kurukshetra. Arjun deviated from his chosen goals and finally gave up his archery in the battlefield. Lord Krishna motivated him and coached through precious sermons which is known as 'Bhagawad Gita' and enlightened Arjun. He said, "Karm kar phal ki chinta mat kar" which means "Action is the duty; reward is not thy concern" which is followed by many in the world. Our duty is to work hard and give our best and the rest will be taken care of God. When we emphasize more on outcomes we tend to lose focus on efforts, thus getting dejected when we don't achieve the desired outcomes. Hence, we must do our duty constantly with an emphasis on excellence by enjoying our journey of life without losing sight of our destination. Lord Krishna asserted that it was always the right that prevails over might and advised Arjun to do duty without looking for returns. He finally prepared Arjun to fight against the wrong people although they were his relatives.

Lord Krishna – A Situational Leader

Lord Krishna was a master strategist and coach with wealth of knowledge and tons of wisdom. He knew how to inspire others with his thought provoking, inspiring and meaningful messages. He was a true leader who adopted various leadership styles as per the situation. He can be called situational leader as he was a democratic, delegative, autocratic, transformational, transactional, and above all, a charismatic leader. He was good at people skills and a great communicator who knew how to influence the human mind to achieve the desired objectives.

Lord Krishna – A Great Coach

Prior to the battle of Kurukshetra, both Duryodan and Arjun approache Lord Krishna to fight on behalf of Kauravas and Pandavas respectively. Lord Krishna offers two options to them whether they would prefer him as a charioteer or a huge army of soldiers. Duryodan prefers a huge army of soldiers to Lord Krishna while Arjun prefers Lord Krishna as a charioteer and coach to a huge army of soldiers. Finally, in the battle of Kurukshetra Pandavas won the battle with Lord Krishna's coaching abilities while the Kauravas lost the battle despite having a huge army of soldiers on their side. It is obvious that a person with great coaching skills and guiding abilities is much superior to an army of soldiers. It shows the significance of coaching as coaches build skills and abilities among the coachees which help the latter build more than an army of soldiers.

It is obvious from this Hindu mythology that the concept of coaching existed since time immemorial but in a different form. It is also a fact that coaching existed across the world where coaches coached the kings. Currently we have CEO coaches like Marshall Goldsmith who is the world's number ranked coach and one of the top ten CEO coaches in the world.

Hire a Coach to Fast-track Your Career

You must hire a coach irrespective of the rank, title or the position you hold in order to grow in your life. A great coach helps you align your energies and strengths with goals and motivates to achieve the desired outcomes and success in your personal, professional and social life. Remember that the tools and techniques that helped you come up to your current position might not help you to reach your next higher position. Hence, equip yourself constantly with necessary innovative tools and techniques to fast-track your career and achieve all-round success.

"A good coach will make his players see what they can become rather than what they are."

– ARA PARSEGHIAN

CHAPTER 34

Help Successful Students Become Even More Successful

"More important than the curriculum is the question of the methods of teaching and the spirit in which the teaching is given."
- BERTRAND RUSSELL

In every classroom, educators often find three levels of students – below average, average, and above average students in terms of their levels of intelligence and understanding the essence. The role of educators must be to ensure that the knowledge reach out to all levels of students equally. It is easier said than done. Therefore, educators must deliver the key ideas and insights three times in the classroom so that all levels of students can understand the essence effectively. When educators tell the key concepts first time, the above average students understand the message. When they tell second time, the average students understand the message. When they tell third time, the below average students understand the message.

The role of educators is to elevate below average students as average students, average students as above average students, and above average students as extraordinary students. Precisely, educators must help successful students become even more successful to provide a meaning to their profession and make a qualitative difference to the lives of students.

> *"There are two kinds of teachers: the kind that fills you with so much quail shot that you can't move, and the kind that just gives you a little prod behind and you jump to the skies."*
>
> - ROBERT FROST

CHAPTER 35

Emotional Intelligence for Educators

"If your emotional abilities aren't in hand, if you don't have self-awareness, if you are not able to manage your distressing emotions, if you can't have empathy and have effective relationships, then no matter how smart you are, you are not going to get very far."
- DANIEL GOLEMAN

Ever since Daniel Goleman came out with Emotional Intelligence (EI) it invited the attention of many people internationally with Google hits of approximately 9.47 million results with diverse contexts, including education, health, relationships and work. There is a growing interest towards EI in all sectors as it is closely associated with leadership. In fact, leadership success and effectiveness mostly depends on EI. There had been a raging debate among various leadership scholars and practitioners whether leaders are born or made. Daniel Goleman's EI cleared the debate and concluded that leaders are made rather born, as EI helps an ordinary person acquire leadership abilities and skills and excel as a leader.

EI is essential in all industries as we need leaders in all sectors. It is also required in the education sector where educators have to handle emotions, feelings and egos of diversified students in the classroom. The educators must be aware of their own emotions and match their emotions with the students' emotions as per the situation to create compatibility and chemistry with the students to ensure effective teaching takeaways. The educators must apply different strokes to different students as all students are not alike in their intelligence levels and learning styles. Students in the classroom usually belong to three categories - above average, average and below average in their intelligence levels. They appreciate various learning styles - auditory, visual and kinesthetic. Hence, the educators must change their teaching style as per the learning styles and the intelligence levels of the students. While delivering their teaching sessions they must take feedback by observing the body language of the students in the classroom and change their teaching methods and strategies accordingly.

To conclude, the educators must take various aspects in view while teaching and training in the classroom i.e. catering as per the intelligence level of students and as per their learning styles with the aid of emotional intelligence to achieve the effective teaching takeaways among the students and excel as effective educators.

> *"People high in emotional intelligence are expected to progress more quickly through the abilities designated and to master more of them."*
>
> — MAYER & SALOVEY

Students Excel Better than their Educators

"Ideal teachers are those who use themselves as bridges over which they invite their students to cross, then having facilitated their crossing, joyfully collapse, encouraging them to create bridges of their own."
- NIKOS KAZANTZAKIS

In one of my leadership training programs a participant asked me a question – why educators cannot grow while some of their students outsmart their educators? In fact, it is a rare question I have come across in my lifetime. I responded as follows:

Educators share their knowledge, ideas and insights with their students. They make a difference in the lives of their students with their passion, knowledge and experience. And the students acquire knowledge from their educators and apply it in their real lives and reap rewards greatly. In fact, the application of knowledge is more important than the acquisition of knowledge. Educators have knowledge and ideas which they may not be able to apply in their lives as their main role is to share knowledge as per the expectations of their students and to make them successful. Hence, they are engaged with their task of creating, generating, and sharing their knowledge with others. On the other hand, the students apply the acquired ideas and insights in a number of areas and reap great rewards. Students work very hard in their lives and finally, make it big and achieve greatness. Therefore, the roles of educators and students are different.

Parents want to see the success of their children. When children succeed the parents are happy since they treat their children's success as their success. Similarly, educators will be happy when they see the success of their students, and they feel that they are successful in their lives. Above all, a true parent's success lies in the success of their children, and a true educator's success lies in the success of their students. To conclude, educators remain as educators while the students outsmart their educators and grow to the level of CEOs and great leaders.

> *"A good teacher is like a candle - it consumes itself to light the way for others."*
>
> *- AUTHOR UNKNOWN*

PART - III

MISCELLANEOUS

CHAPTER 37

Unsuccessful Parents and Successful Children

"The words a father speaks to his children in the privacy of the home are not overheard at the time, but, as in whispering galleries, they will be clearly heard at the end and by posterity."
- JEAN PAUL RICHTER

It has been observed that the parents who failed in business or life tend to be more cautious and secretive by nature. They often don't appreciate revealing their cards, and are more responsible and careful in their decision-making. They empathize with others. They take more precautions in bringing up their children so that the latter can avoid repeating such mistakes. They micromanage their children and observe every moment so that children grow safely to succeed in this competitive world. The ultimate aim of such parents is to see the success in their children as they could not taste success in their lifetimes.

Unsuccessful fathers protect their children to ensure safety. In such scenario the children grow more comfortable and confident; and they exhibit self-control and maturity. The unsuccessful fathers monitor the performance of their children from time to time to keep children from getting out of the track. They encourage their children to come out of their comfort zones. When children do well they raise the bar constantly so that children grow competitive and collaborative in their lives. In fact, failed fathers are the real leadership trainers for their children in life.

The children of unsuccessful parents are more realistic and understand the problems at the grass root level. They emphasize more on ideas rather than brooding over issues and individuals. They are highly focused and understand the harsh realities in life. They are more careful and are determined to taste success to make their parents proud. They become tougher mentally and don't get weighed down by the failures in their lives since they learned lessons from the experiences of their parents. They often learn from the experiences of others to avoid getting trapped. And they quickly learn lessons when they make mistakes in their lives. They take both success and failure with equanimity. They empathize with others and grow as responsible citizens and successful persons ultimately. Hence, their success is definitely is higher and laudable.

God is great as He balances the account statement with successes and failures. If parents fail during their lifetime He compensates by blessing success to their children. Hence, both failed parents and their children don't have to regret for failures as life is full of peaks and valleys and life is incomplete without ups and downs. To conclude, the failed fathers are more cautious towards their children while their children are more determined to achieve success.

"We must do all that we can, to give our children the best in education and social upbringing - for while they are the youth of today, they shall be the leaders of tomorrow."

- JOHN F. KENNEDY

CHAPTER 38

Women Appreciate Men who are Persistent

"Through sources, we have obtained the following alien assessment of the human species: The male wants to be valued for what he pretends to be. The female wants to be overvalued for what she truly is."
- ROBERT BRAULT

Success can be compared with a woman as achieving success is not easy, and winning the heart of a woman is equally not easy. When you want to achieve success you have to slog hard through various tools and techniques, and means and methods. In fact, there is one difference between success and failure – persistence. Those who persist are bound to succeed. Most of the inventions occurred due to the persistence by inventors. Thomas Edison failed more than 1000 times in inventing the light bulb. Alexander Graham Bell failed many times in inventing the telephone. When you look at legendary entrepreneur Colonel Sanders who failed many times, and finally succeeded in setting up KFC in his old age. It was all due to his persistent efforts. Similarly, if you want to win the heart of a woman you must persist with a sincere and pure heart. When a woman is convinced that you truly love her through your persistent efforts she would trust your love and appreciate your persistence. Hence, if you fail to win the heart of a woman next time, don't give up. Keep trying with a pure heart, and one day she would fall in love with you. Remember the American proverb, "A man chases a woman until she catches him."

Good luck with your success and sweet heart!

"To get to a woman's heart, a man must first use his own."
- MIKE DOBBERTIN

CHAPTER 39

We all were Born from the Wombs of Women

"The thing women have yet to learn is nobody gives you power.
You just take it."
- ROSEANNE BARR

Currently there are frequent reports of rapes of women. The atrocities on women are on the rise. In 2012, a woman was gang-raped in the midnight in a moving bus in Delhi which drew attention across India. It indicates that there is no safety for the women in independent India. It shows the way men treat and commodify women in their real lives. Some people blame cinema and media as being responsible for such atrocities being committed on women. In fact, cinema provides entertainment and media spreads information. Hence, it is something beyond cinema and media.

Rape is a sexual assault on opposite sex without any consent. It happens usually on women by men, and in rare cases it happens on men by women. Rape is an inhuman and cruel act. It is a brutal invasion of a woman's space and freedom. Rapists are beasts without any rational and logical mind. They go by animal instincts to fulfill their sexual desires by any means.

Let us appreciate the fact that it is natural for a politician to show his powers; a wealthy man to exhibit his wealth; a knowledgeable man to demonstrate his wisdom; an artist to show his talent; a sportsperson to show his skills; and a beautiful woman to show her beauty. These are all natural tendencies among human beings. But people should never think of grabbing such things without their permission. They can work hard, smart and wise and acquire them through an ethical and acceptable social behavior.

Id, Ego and Super Ego

It is deplorable that Swamis and male chauvinists blame women for moving in the midnight and wearing indecent attire. There are other reasons responsible for such incidents. According to the noted psychologist, Sigmund Freud, the human mind is trifurcated into three compartments - Id, Ego and Super Ego. Id is instinctive and irrational; Ego is rational and logical; and Super Ego is ethical and moral. Id can be compared with a demon; Ego can be compared with a human being; and Super Ego can be compared with an angel. Hence, Ego is the human being carrying the demon of Id on one side of the shoulder and the angel of Super Ego on the other side of the shoulder. Every man encounters these three stages every time. He will be rational and logical when he is able to crush his irrational and instinctive – Id, and allows it to be overtaken by Ego. If he allows it further, he will appreciate from ethical angle and stand out from others as a role-model. When we look at rapes on women, it is the Id which is responsible for such instant and instinctive inhuman acts. Although desire to have sex is a natural one for every human being, the human mind must think logically and rationally since it is essential to have consent of opposite sex to mate. But sometimes men are instigated in the wrong company of friends and resort to such heinous acts. At the same time, women must understand the basic body language to convey right signals to others in public place. Some women don't realize that they send tempting signals to others unconsciously from their body language. Mistaking such signals as welcoming gestures, men resort to such inhuman acts resulting in untold trauma.

Remedial Measures

Parental upbringing matters a lot to check atrocities on women and prevent rapes. Parents must teach their children how to behave with fairer sex. Non Governmental Organizations can take active part in helping the victims; checking the atrocities on women; and highlighting such brutal acts to serve as deterrent. Men must empathize that they were born to women. They should not get intoxicated by irrational and instant sexual temptations.

Women must take precautions to defend from such rogues by mastering the basics of martial arts and using them at an appropriate time to defend themselves. They can also send message through their cell phones to police to get timely assistance when they sense that some untoward incident is going to take place. They must also learn the basics of body language that tempt men to resort to rape. The existing Indian laws are not enough, and hence, it is time to plug the loopholes in the law to avert such incidents. Government must provide more security cover to women. Men's perception towards women must change. There must be a drastic change in the mindsets of men towards women that should help to respect and treat women with dignity.

Conclusion

Indian men must not treat women as sexual objects. They must respect the egos, emotions and feelings of women. They must empathize with women. Before advancing a woman with evil intentions men must think a number of times about the women in their family. If they think in that way, and empathize with women the atrocities on women will come down.

Swami Vivekananda rightly said, "All nations have attained greatness by paying proper respect to women." Hence, let us respect women to attain greatness. Let us not forget that we all were born from the wombs of women.

"Life on the planet is born of woman."

\- ADRIENNE RICHE

CHAPTER 40

Add Value to Soar Like an Eagle

"When you cease to make a contribution, you begin to die."
- ELEANOR ROOSEVELT

The Gen Y is much smarter than Gen X and the Baby Boomers. They have lots of fire, and are highly ambitious. They are more intelligent than their previous generation, and are determined to leave a mark behind for others to follow. However, they must exercise patience and think critically about their goals to achieve them successfully. Here are the questions the Gen Y and Indian students must ponder to achieve big in their lives:

Do you know who you are?

Do you understand what you are doing?

Do you recognize that you have a huge potential?

Do you spot your strengths and weaknesses?

Do you know the meaning of your life?

Do you introspect and consider the fundamental philosophical and metaphysical questions?

Do you add value to yourself?

Do you add value to your parents?

Do you add value to your educators?

Do you add value to your society?

Do you add value to your country?

Do you add value to your world?

Do you know that you are rightly placed in Indian history?

Do you know that there are ample employment opportunities?

Do you know that you face the challenge of unemployability rather than unemployment in India?

Do you know that Indian youth constitute more than 50 per cent of the population?

Do you know that you have the power to make India a super power?

Think! When you think you will identify ample of opportunities for growth and expansion. Emphasize on means, not ends. Don't go by shortcut as it will cut you short. Be ambitious; don't be overambitious. Love your community, don't hate others' community. Think. Identify. Explore. Expand. You were born to achieve big in this world!

Soar Like an Eagle!

Eagle is an exceptional bird that can convert threats into opportunities. It prefers to eat fresh meat rather than stale meat. It wants the best of everything in life. It undergoes tons of trials and tribulations during its lifetime and leads from the front. It can fly high at a height of 5 kilometers and look at the objects from a long distance. It is a visionary. Hence, eagle is compared with leader because of its unique features and leadership abilities. To conclude, lead from the front and soar like an eagle.

"The foundation of every state is the education of its youth."

- Diogenes Laertius

"When I stand before God at the end of my life, I would hope that I would not have a single bit of talent left, and could say, "I used everything you gave me.""

- Erma Bombeck

References

http://www.facebook.com/pages/Professor-MSRao/451516514937414?skip_nax_wizard=true
http://speakermix.com/professor-m-s-rao
Author's Blogs:
http://professormsraoguru.blogspot.com
http://professormsrao.blogspot.com
http://profmsr.blogspot.com

Are You a Left-Brainer or a Right-Brainer?

"Your incredible brain can take you from rags to riches, from loneliness to popularity, and from depression to happiness and joy - if you use it properly."
- BRIAN TRACY

If you want to achieve success smartly and quickly, being aware of your strengths and weaknesses helps you reap rewards greatly. When you identify your strengths you will be able to exploit them to achieve your desired objectives. When you know your weaknesses you can correct yourself quickly whenever you make mistakes and you can also gradually overcome them through practice. In addition, if you are aware about yourself whether you are a left-brainer or right-brainer you can make use of your strengths and grow quickly in all spheres of your life.

According to Nobel Laureate, Roger W. Sperry, human brain is divided into two compartments (hemispheres) – left-brain and right-brain. Some people use more of left-brain, some use more of right-brain and a few use whole-brain. In fact, human mind is very powerful. If you know about yourself whether you are left-brainer or right-brainer you can make use of your mind, and be able to unlock your hidden potential to achieve a huge success in your life.

Research shows that those who are "right-brained" are said to be more intuitive, thoughtful and subjective while those who are "left-brained" are often said to be more logical, analytical and objective. The left-brainers are more logical and have an eye for detail. They can become good writers and researchers. They are also good at language. Hence, they can also become good speakers. Precisely, they are down-to-earth. In contrast, the right-brainers are highly imaginative and creative and can thrive on risk. Succinctly, they appreciate spatial perception and can see the big picture. They can think out-of-the box and become scientists and excel as inventors.

Left-brainers are logical, rational and sequential and prefer to work alone in a quiet place while the right-brainers are intuitive and simultaneously prefer to work in teams. The left-brainers are systematic and well-structured people and possess more of technical acumen. They appreciate everything that is well organized. They don't liko distractions. In contrast, the right-brainers have social acumen. And the left-brainer may become a right-brainer or vice versa as per the changing times and their age and experiences.

Choose Your Career

The left-brainers can opt for careers that have less interaction with others and can work alone such as clerk, librarian, accountant, advisor, engineer, banker, counselor, and programmer to name a few. The right-brainers can opt for careers that have more interaction and can involve group activities such as director, designer, instructor, consultant, trainer, and psychologist. The left-brainers prefer to work indoors and appreciate using more of their mental energies and less of physical energies while the right-brainers prefer to work outdoors using more of their physical energies and less of mental energies. The left-brainers prefer to work in serene place while the right-brainers prefer to work in a noisy environment.

It is good if you use both sides of your brain to uncork your hidden potential. Realizing your brain type helps you identify your strengths and gradually make a shift to use your brain holistically to achieve all-round success in your life.

You can take online tests to know whether you are a left-brainer or a right-brainer. Here is another way to find out whether you are left-brainer or right-brainer: When you watch a dancer and if you see in the clockwise direction, then you use more of the right-brain. In contrast, if you see the dancer in the anti-clockwise direction, then you use more of the left-brain. Next time, when you watch dancing observe yourself keenly as you not only enjoy dancing and also analyze yourself whether you are left-brainer or right-brainer.

> *"Don't limit yourself. Many people limit themselves to what they think they can do. You can go as far as your mind lets you. What you believe, you can achieve."*
>
> - MARY KAY ASH

Right or Left-Brainer Test

Here is a test to know whether you are a left-brainer or right-brainer. Answer these questions to find out the same:

1. Which hand do you write with normally?
2. Which hand do you eat?
3. Take a step. Which foot did you use?
4. Which hand do you use when brushing your teeth?
5. Which hand do you open a cola bottle with?

If you answered left to these questions, you are normally right-brained. If you answered right to most questions, you are usually left-brained. If it's a mixed result, you could be more whole-brained.

Reference

http://www.essortment.com/am-right-brained-left-brained 43337.html

'Play and Learn' Method – An Innovative Learning Tool

"Do not train children to learning by force and harshness, but direct them to it by what amuses their minds, so that you may be better able to discover with accuracy the peculiar bent of the genius of each."
- PLATO

Presently most of the Indian youth think that education is a burden, not an enlightenment. They think that the present education system is outdated as it emphasizes on assignments and exams, not on creativity and innovation. It emphasizes more on qualifications, not on knowledge. It emphasizes more on theory, not on application. In this appendix, I am going to address categories of students and introduce an innovative learning tool - 'Play and Learn' Method that helps students discover the joy of learning and ensure effective learning outcomes.

We can classify students into two categories. First category of students pursues education to please their parents and well-wishers; and the second category of students pursues education to acquire knowledge and apply in their real lives. Find out which category you belong?

Some of the students in the second category emphasize on scores and grades to grab employment opportunities. Some students learn concepts to apply in their real lives. The rest of the students have appetite to acquire knowledge. In fact, this set of students stand out from others as they get good grades, apply knowledge and provide meaning to life. They achieve greatly in the long-run although they may encounter hiccups academically in the short-term.

The students who're not comfortable with the present education system must adopt new learning tools and techniques to acquire knowledge and score good grades in exams. For instance, the 'Play and Learn' method works well for such students. Here is how this method goes:

Adopt 5 I Approach

This innovative learning tool is a five-fold process of investigating, imagining, intuiting, integrating and inferring the entire content while reading. The learners must investigate about the topic or the subject they read. They must question themselves why they are reading the content. They must imagine the content logically and read between the lines to acquire the essence. They must intuit the information analytically and integrate it holistically. Finally, they must infer the essence to ensure knowledge retention for a long duration. Precisely, take a particular topic you find it tough to understand, and then break it into small portions. Take each portion, observe the words that are easy and make a note of them.

Represent them in an arrow format to understand and retain the information easily. The following diagram describes the method elaborately:

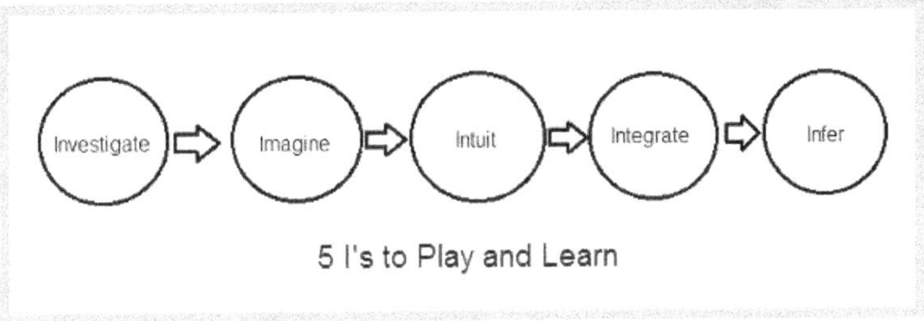

Figure 1

Advantages of 'Play and Learn' Method

"Learning without thought is labor lost; thought without learning is perilous."

\- CONFUCIUS

- This method helps you understand the content quickly.
- It overcomes the challenges in the present Indian education which follows 3Rs – Read, Write and Reproduce.
- Everyone has their limitations while learning. This learning tool helps them broaden their conceptual skills and improves mind power.
- Students with below average intelligence should adopt 'Play and Learn' method and educators too should adopt 'Play and Teach' method.

- 'Play and Teach' is similar to the learning tool. The educators who can't get things right on the subject should adopt this style.

Hence, students must find out new learning tools constantly to understand effectively and retain the knowledge for a long time to enjoy the fruits of learning. Above all, they must emphasize on acquisition and application of knowledge to excel as leaders.

> *"Learning and innovation go hand in hand. The arrogance of success is to think that what you did yesterday will be sufficient for tomorrow."*
>
> – WILLIAM POLLARD

Reference

Blog: http://mgshyd.wordpress.com

Acknowledgement

I acknowledge the contribution of my brother, Meka Ramakrishna Sayee, in the development of the innovative learning tool, 'Play and Learn' Method.

Freshers' Concerns and Clarifications

"Curiosity has its own reason for existence. The important thing is not to stop questioning."
- ALBERT EINSTEIN

Here is a list of concerns with clarifications and questions with answers about jobs, career, success, personality development and leadership for freshers:

Q: How to develop positive attitude?

A: When you set your goals your mind will be highly focused. It removes negative thoughts from your mind and replaces with positive thoughts. It helps you manage your time and build positive attitude.

Q: How can you differentiate between positive and negative attitude?

A: A person with a positive attitude always thinks of winning and staying ahead of others whereas the person with a negative attitude always thinks of pulling down others. When you look at Barack Obama you find that he has a positive attitude. In contrast, Osama Bin Laden had a negative attitude. Remember, it is the people with positive attitude who win at the end although they encounter several challenges during the course of their life journey.

Q: Is it good to have negative attitude in exceptional cases?

A: No. Although the righteous man falls 10 times he rises but the wicked man never falls twice. God supports people with good intentions even if they fail many times. But He never supports the people with bad intentions. That means there is no second chance for wicked people.

Q: How do you make your mind strong psychologically?

A: Hold your mind for 21 seconds with positive thoughts and do it for 21 days. You will be able to develop a strong mind over a period of time.

Q: How do you define personality?

A: Personality is all about how you carry yourself - your appearance, behavior, attitude, etiquette and presentation to name a few. Your personality depends on three factors – heredity, environment and situation.

Q: How can you improve your behavior?

A: Your attitude will reflect your behavior. If you have positive attitude then you develop positive behavior. Hence, build positive attitude to find behavioral improvements within you.

Q: How do you spot your talents?

A: Find out the areas in which you are more interested. The activities in which you are more interested indicate your talents. There is a personality test – MBTI (Myers-Briggs Type Indicator) which reveals 16 personality types. When you take this test you will understand which personality type you belong and the careers that are suitable to you. Hence, take this test to spot your talents and also the careers that are close to your heart.

Q: What is the difference between aim and goal?

A: Aim is to try something for time being but goal is something you try with a roadmap, deadline, impact and influence. Aim is to look at the things in order to achieve it while goal is a blueprint with short-term and long-term strategies to accomplish it.

Q: How can I reach my goals quickly?

A: Set SMART goals where SMART is the acronym for specific, measurable, achievable, reachable and trackable. For instance, if you want to become a class I officer in the central government, you must specify which area you want to enter. You must be able to measure how long it takes to reach. Assess whether you can achieve it or not. Find out whether it is realistic or not. Finally, track your status of reaching the goals from time to time by taking feedback. In addition, divide your goals into short-term and long-term and align them constantly to accomplish your goals.

Q: Why do students change their goals?

A: In a country like India, students set their goals due to parental and peer pressure. As a result, they quickly change their goals when they don't accomplish. When you want to achieve your goals you must first look at your passions and talents and then set goals accordingly. Once you set you must proceed with energy and enthusiasm. There will be obstacles in the journey but you must overcome them successfully. Remember, not to change your destination but only change your means to reach your destination.

Q: How do I judge whether I can achieve my goal?

A: You must take inventory of your talents and skills and check your confidence levels to accomplish your goals.

Q: Is it better to focus on short-term goals or long-term goals?

A: Divide your goals into short-term and long-term goals and align them. Even if there is a failure to reach your short-term goals, your long-term goals will help you stay motivated.

Q: How can I face the interview board with confidence?

A: Before you attend interview, check prospective company's profile from various sources. Find out their vision and mission statements. Prepare a few questions likely to be asked during interview. You will be able to respond with confidence.

Q: What do the interviewers look at during interview?

A: The employers look for various skills which can be summarized as mindset, toolset and skill set. You can compare the same with attitude, hard skills and soft skills respectively.

Q: Is it necessary to be honest during interview?

A: Yes. You must be honest and tactful during interview to grab the employment offer.

Q: Is attitude alone enough to get employment offer?

A: In fact, you need to project a right mindset, toolset and skill set to get the employment offer. Attitude plays a crucial role apart from others skills that you possess. Mindset is attitude, toolset is all about eligibility like qualifications and skill set is about suitability like competencies. When you can blend them effectively you will find better employment prospects.

Q: How can the recruiters believe that I have an attitude?

A: Recruiters are experts to spot whether you have attitude or not. Sometimes there may be a psychologist in the group interview who will assess your attitude. When you speak you must come out with examples and anecdotes that show your conviction and convey the message to the recruiters.

Q: What will you do if we don't recruit you?

A: I will try elsewhere.

Q: What will you do if you don't get job?

A: I will pursue higher studies and keep searching for jobs.

Q: Can I ask my roles and responsibilities during interview?

A: When you apply for a job you must have clarity in your mind about the kind of job you have applied. However, when you find any ambiguity about your roles and responsibilities, you can have them clarified to avoid getting stressed out in the workplace with a wrong job.

Q: Can I specify the job I would like to do after reporting?

A: The employer recruits you for a specific job and you need to do that. Be clear about your roles and responsibilities before joining to avoid nightmare at the workplace.

Q: How to get out of negative people while reaching goals?

A: When you are convinced that there are people with negative energies around you, you must get out such zone quickly. If you feel that there is no way to avoid, ignore them.

Q: How to get out of stage fear during presentation?

A: Before you go for delivering your presentation do the following actions: Do light exercises. Do breathing exercises that allows more oxygen go inside your brain and relaxes your mind. Drink water as it cools your body system. Count from 1 to 10 and from 10 to 1 within your mind. Above all, be confident in what you do.

Q: How to develop confidence in delivering presentations?

A: First, start with a small audience and take their feedback to improve yourself. Do research, structure the content and share it in a piecemeal manner. Practice by speaking one sentence by looking at one person and then speak second sentence by looking at the face of the second person. Shift your eye contact from one person to another person in this way for each sentence. Over a period of time you maintain eye contact with all people in the audience with confidence. It requires a lot of practice to build confidence to deliver presentations.

Q: What will you do when you get blank while delivering presentation?

A: Drink water and by then you can recollect your ideas. Or ask any one of the participants to summarize what you said. You would be able to recall by this time to continue with your presentation.

Q: What do you mean by regional celebrity?

A: The person who is prominent at the regional level or local level with visibility and good number of followers is known as regional celebrity.

Q: What is the difference between smart and hard work

A: Hard work is about efficiency while smart work is about effectiveness. Hard work delivers quantitative outcomes while smart work delivers qualitative outcomes. In order to succeed in this competitive world, you must believe in hard work, smart work and network. And when you blend your hard work and smart work it is known as wise work.

Q: How to develop lateral thinking?

A: Edward De Bono highlighted 'lateral thinking'. When you follow the road less travelled you develop lateral thinking. When you think-out-of the box, you develop it. When you go to college through a different route than the normal route you mind things more actively and thinks from a new perspective. Precisely, when you emphasize on different healthy means to reach your goals then you develop lateral thinking.

Q: Was Osama a good leader?

A: No. He was a bad leader who created havoc by masterminding the attack on twin towers in America. A good leader uses his intelligence, abilities and skills for the benefit of mankind. He never terrorizes and causes destruction. Hence, Osama was a bad leader.

Q: Do I have to depend on my native language or on English?

A: Both. It is always advisable to learn more languages to fast-track your career and avail the opportunities available internationally.

Q: How to manage time?

A: Follow ABCDE of time management. A stands for urgent and important; B stands for not urgent but important; C stands for neither important nor urgent but you have to do the tasks; D stands for delegation; and E stands for elimination. For instance, when you have ten tasks to execute, categorize them into ABCDE and you will be able to manage your time effectively.

Q: Does a technical person require to know corporate life before joining the company?

A: You must know basics of corporate life and etiquette and the rest is taught to you by the companies during their induction programs and you learn when you work in the company.

Q: How to become a CEO quickly?

A: It requires a lengthy response. However, I would like to condense in a few words. You must follow your passions. You must not change jobs frequently. You must emphasize more on EQ (Emotional Quotient) rather than on IQ (Intelligence Quotient). You must have a global mindset and possess more of conceptual skills than that of hard and soft skills. Above all, you have to learn, unlearn and relearn with changing times and technologies to become a CEO quickly.

Q: Is it good to consult others before we make decisions?

A: It depends on the nature of the person, position and the issue. All you must do is to blend your head, heart and gut to make a decision. But here is a caution that all decisions might not go right as some fall flat. You must learn lessons from your failures and bounce back.

Q: Does everyone look for career?

A: There is a difference between job and career. When people enter into employment for money it is known as job. When people enter into employment beyond money with a long-term vision it is known as career. Currently most of the students are ambitious and they prefer to pursue careers rather than jobs.

Q: Do all students who have been recruited by companies have the right attitude?

A: Majority of them possess the right attitude. However, in rare cases candidates with rotten attitude enter into employment as no system is accurate. There are bound to be some mistakes in recruitment.

Q: What is the difference between businessman and tycoon?

A: Businessman is someone who does commercial transactions to make money. A small trader is also a businessman. In contrast, tycoon is someone who sets up Business Empire like Richard Branson and Laxmi Niwas Mittal.

Q: How to maintain a poker face?

A: Don't exhibit your feelings and emotions externally. Try to control through your mind to stay cool and calm.

Q: How to control emotions?

A: Relax yourself. You can do yoga or meditation that helps you control your emotions.

Q: How to overcome depression?

A: Hold your thoughts for 21 seconds with positive mindset and you can overcome depression.

Q: How to motivate myself?

A: Always be with positive people who value and respect you. It is natural for human beings to experience peaks and valleys. Whenever you experience valleys your friends will encourage you to come out of them as you are always with positive people who help you to stay motivated. You can also read motivational books that lift your energy levels.

Q: Why did you post interview questions in your blog?

A: To help my students. I am passionate about my students and I have passion to share my knowledge with the world. I want to dedicate my rest of my life for training people to become great leaders and organizations to become great ones. Hence, I created three blogs for three kinds of audiences that are read widely in the world. Here are the links:

http://professormsrao.blogspot.com,
http://professormsraoguru.blogspot.com and
http://profmsr.blogspot.com Here is my speaker mix link:
http://speakermix.com/professor-m-s-rao

Q: How can I change my behavior?

A: When you condition your mind you will be able to change your behavior the way you want. You can give positive commands to yourself that get reinforced in your subconscious mind thus reflecting in your behavior over a period of time.

Q: How to remove misunderstanding with others?

A: Most of the problems in the world are due to excessive ego and miscommunication. Hence, talk to the person with whom you have misunderstanding so that you will be able to look from other person's perspective. If you have made any mistakes, apologize and restart your relations. Life is very short. Therefore, make it sweet.

Q: How to come out of setbacks quickly?

A: Find out the root of the problem, learn lessons and move forward. Don't brood over your past mistakes. Research has shown that people waste 30 percent of their time by thinking about their unpleasant past that cannot be changed. Mistakes are an integral part of life and make a better person and successful person if you learn from them.

Q: Which one should I pursue between job and higher education?

A: It depends on your financial muscle. If you are financially strong go for higher studies. If there are no funds, go in for a job and pursue higher studies.

Q: In group discussion, does the first speaker get credit?

A: Opening participant has an advantage over others as s/he has points to speak and sometimes may not develop clarity quickly. In the meanwhile, other participants develop some clarity on the topic and be able to speak with confidence. And the last participants may not have any points to speak as most of the points have been covered by the other participants.

Q: What happens when some participants don't allow others to speak?

A: Such participants send wrong signals to the moderator and get negative marks. Hence, it is ideal to encourage non-participants to participant in the group discussion.

Q: I want to achieve success all the times in my life. Is it possible?

A: No. It is not possible. Every man fails in life at some point of life. Failure is an integral part of life and the law of the nature. But be mentally prepared to face the challenges to achieve success.

Q: Why are half of the students good and the rest half are not good in the classroom?

A: Indian education encourages rote learning – 3 Rs - read, write and reproduce. Students don't read entire book but they read only a few questions to score in the exams. There must be a change in the mindset of the students to acquire knowledge rather than score high in exams as qualifications get them employment, but knowledge keep them firmly on their feet.

Q: Should I speak in English with great vocabulary?

A: The objective of any communication is to reach out to the audience. Hence, use simple, straight and plain language that the other person understands and appreciates.

Q: What is the difference between responding and reacting?

A: Responding is positive while reacting is negative.

Q: Are average people better than the above average people?

A: Yes. In some aspects, not in all aspects.

Q: Which is more important – knowledge or experience?

A: Both are important. Knowledge helps gain experience and experience equips you with knowledge and teaches many lessons in life.

Q: Is it good to escape when other person is strong?

A: No. You have to face the strong person one day. Believe in strength, not size. When you read the biblical story of David versus Goliath, David was a small in size who took on the mighty Goliath and killed him. When you look at Singapore it is a small country but a prosperous one despite not being blessed with natural resources. Hence, don't bother about size. Believe in yourself and face the challenges squarely.

Q: Why could Socrates not earn money though he was such a great philosopher?

A: Everyone is not after money. Every person has different needs and works accordingly. You need to give different strokes to different people. Socrates was a great philosopher who believed in knowledge acquisition, not money acquisition. People are after money, love, knowledge, power etc.; Socrates was after knowledge and excelled as a great philosophor. If he had concentrated on money he would have remained like any other common man. In my personal life, I am rich in heart but poor in pocket. But I enjoy doing the job by sharing my knowledge with others.

Q: Can you develop will power?

A: There are certain things acquired through heredity. For instance, X factor is an inborn quality. Hence, developing will power is a challenging one.

Q: How to get out of stress?

A: There are two types of stress – eustress and distress. When you get the best out of the stress, it is known as eustress and when you get the worst out of the stress, it is known as distress. To get out of stress, take meals at regular intervals, hit gymnasium or go for walking. There are three symptoms of good health - free bowel movement, good appetite and sound health. When you have these things then you are healthy.

Q: When companies don't want to know personal life of employees why do they ask personal details before recruitment?

A: Every company does background verification check to find out the credentials of the candidates. It is a routine exercise not aimed at digging the personal life of the candidates. Companies want to cross check the furnished information by the candidates to have long-term association.

Q: Can a man excel without having any foundation?

A: Yes. It is possible through fire, passion and will power. When you look at Abraham Lincoln and Barack Obama they are amazing examples of leaders who rose from humble origins. In my personal life, I rarely studied in educational institutions from degree onwards. But I earned my BSc, MA, MBA, PGDCLL, and PGDBM through distance mode, and finally acquired my PhD in Soft Skills through my passion for continuous learning. Having strong background is an asset, and not having is not a liability.

Q: Can I close my eyes in the classroom and learn the things?

A: No. You need to maintain eye contact with the speaker to learn in the classroom because you can see the body language gestures which contains 55 percent of communication, others being 7 percent oral language and 38 percent voice modulation. Above all, 'a picture is worth thousand words' goes the saying. Hence, keep open your eyes and ears in the classroom to acquire knowledge.

Q: Why do graduates from other disciplines opt for MBA degree?

A: Anybody can pursue MBA degree to hone their managerial and leadership skills irrespective of the discipline they come from. It helps them manage and lead effectively and quickens their careers success.

Q: What to do when some people simply communicate and achieve success without having any stuff?

A: Such people will not last long. Remember what Abraham Lincoln quoted, "You can fool all the people some of the time, and some of the people all tho time, but you cannot fool all the people all the time." In fact, you must possess hard and soft skills to achieve success in life and any deficiency in one of them creates imbalance among the individuals.

Q: Is it good to be a big fish in a big pond, and is it possible to be a big fish in a big pond?

A: When you are a big fish in a big pond you will come out of your comfort zone and enter into effective zone. You will be with sharks and the best will come out of you. I always stay in effective zone and when effective zone becomes a comfort zone I shift to further higher effective zone. Hence, it is possible to be a big fish in a big pond.

Q: Can a leader escape from his mistakes by saying 'sorry'?

A: Yes. It is not escaping but partly owning responsibility for their mistakes. We are human beings and make mistakes in our daily life. When we realize that we have made mistakes it is better to admit openly and move on without any regrets.

Q: How can I convert my hobby into passion during my employment?

A: After completion of your working hours pursue your hobbies either in the evening leisure time or weekends. If you make money out of it, it is known as moonlighting. Once you are confident of managing resources to sustain yourself you can resign from your regular job and start your own way to make it fulltime with your hobbies.

Q: What is the meaning of 'dignity'?

A: It is all how one maintains. It is connected with self-esteem. When you undervalue yourself you will have inferiority complex and when you overvalue yourself you will have superiority complex. You have to value yourself and value others as well. Love yourself and respect yourself.

Q: Is it right to judge people only by their appearance?

A: We have to judge people holistically, not by taking one or two factors or facets of personality. Dress sense is something to connect with others and people are judged by their inner character and potential.

Q: Why do Indian parents not allow their children to pursue entrepreneurship?

A: Indian society doesn't provide social security measures. Parents don't want their children to take risk to avoid further challenges in their old age. Hence, parents want their children to play safe by going for employment. However, we find a changing trend among students to pursue entrepreneurship.

Q: Who will be recruited by HR – someone with higher score in academics but with less communication skills or lower score with higher communication skills?

A: It depends on the requirement of the company. However, HR recruits the candidates who have judicious mix of scores and communication skills. For any entry level, the HR may consider more of grades and less of communication skills as communication skills can be acquired at the corporate world as the professional ambience teaches them several skills.

Q: Is it correct that when we join in any company the knowledge of what we learned in college is not useful?

A: Mostly correct. College education provides you basic knowledge. After recruitment company will train you as per the needs of their clients. But what you learned in the educational institution serves as an infrastructure while what you build in the company serves you as a superstructure.

Q: Is being a slow learner a liability?

A: No. Many great scientists and inventors including Edition, Einstein, and Charles Darwin are slow learners but they had high imagination and succeeded due to their persistence.

Q: Is imagination more important than knowledge?

A: It was said by Einstein. Imagination creates more knowledge and imagination is unlimited while knowledge is limited. Hence, imagination is more important than knowledge.

Q: Is it good to change job for a better company?

A: Don't change job for petty offers but change only for pretty offers. Job-hopping is not appreciated in the corporate world. Those who are loyal to the companies find better prospects and can fast-track their careers. Research has shown that most of the CEOs are elevated within the company with employee engagement and loyalty.

Q: What are the qualities required to grow quickly?

A: It depends on the type of industry or the sector you get into. Every industry has its own needs. However, there are certain qualities that help fast-track your career. They are: attitude, soft skills, communication skills, team building skills, leadership skills, emotional intelligence, flexibility and adaptability to name a few.

Q: How can you differentiate between formal and informal behavior?

A: Formal behavior needs basic etiquette including dress code. It is all about professional approach. In contrast, informal behavior is a casual approach that often takes place among the peers.

Q: What is endurance and can you give some examples?

A: It is the ability to bounce back from shocks and setbacks. It is the ability to ensure smart comeback. A leader like Abraham Lincoln is an amazing example of one who failed a number of times, endured several shocks and setbacks, and finally, succeeded in becoming the first Republican President of America.

Q: What is win-win?

A: It is an ideal situation where all stakeholders are happy with the outcome of a conflict. Win-win is about collaboration rather than competing, compromising, accommodating and avoiding, and it is compared with an owl.

Q: When a question is posed I respond and then think that I would have responded better. How to respond better in the first attempt itself?

A: That means you have an attitude for excellence. Everyone speaks spontaneously but a few people think subsequently that they would have delivered better. They think through and restructure their mind and deliver. It is known as excellence.

Q: If I present more during interview does it appear like boosting?

A: Boosting means telling more than what you have. Instead you must show your strengths. In interview, you have to sell out yourself to grab the employment opportunity. Therefore, present what you have to come out with flying colors.

Q: How to maintain work-life balance?

A: Follow the principle of 8-8-8 hours where you spend 8 hours to sleep, 8 hours to work and 8 hours for other activities including personal and social life. Precisely, balance your personal, professional and social life to avoid regrets at the end of your life.

Q: How to start an NGO?

A: Create a common cause, persuade the people to join and conduct meetings regularly by spreading your vision. More and more people join and the organization takes off gradually. Invite dignitaries to bring greater awareness to add value and enhance visibility. Over a period of time, it gets noticed and you can start making a difference.

Q: Is it necessary to be educated when we want to pursue our passions?

A: Yes. Education is not basically for employment but for getting along with society and to have basic knowledge of various aspects. Education is for empowerment and enlightenment. Education helps you face challenges in life and you can stand firmly on your feet. After acquiring basic graduation you can pursue anything as you feel like. If things don't work out in your area of passion you can go for employment as you have basic qualification to work anywhere to earn your bread.

Q: Why cannot youth lead the country?

A: Only youth can lead this country, not older generation. India constitutes more than 50 percent of young population who must take country forward. In India, politicians bring divisions between religions, regions, languages or castes. People are often easily incited by such unscrupulous politicians. Hence, youth should not fall prey to such politicians. They must come forward to lead from the front.

Q: What is your message to students?

A: Work hard, work smart, and work wise. Build your network and grow. There are ample opportunities currently. You must identify the opportunities and grab them to take things forward. Love your mother but don't hate another person's mother.

"The biggest mistake that you can make is to believe that you are working for somebody else. Job security is gone. The driving force of a career must come from the individual. Remember: Jobs are owned by the company, you own your career!" - Earl Nightingale

References
http://www.facebook.com/pages/Professor-MSRao/451516514937414?skip_nax_wizard=true
http://speakermix.com/professor-m-s-rao
Author's Blogs:
http://professormsraoguru.blogspot.com
http://professormsrao.blogspot.com
http://profmsr.blogspot.com

References

Leadership: Ambition--Vice or Virtue? by John Baldoni

Effective Learning by Alan Mumford

Online References

Author's Facebook Page:
http://www.facebook.com/pages/Professor-MSRao/451516514937414?skip_nax_wizard=true

Author's Speaker Mix: http://speakermix.com/professor-m-s-rao

Author's Speaker Mix: http://speakermix.com/m-ganesh-sai

Author's Blog: http://profmsr.blogspot.com

Author's Blog: http://professormsrao.blogspot.com

Author's Blog: http://professormsraoguru.blogspot.com

Author's Blog: http://mgshyd.wordpress.com

http://www.essortment.com/am-right-brained-left-brained-43337.html

Epilogue

"Twenty years from now you will be more disappointed by the things that you didn't do than by the ones you did do. So throw off the bowlines. Sail away from the safe harbor. Catch the trade winds in your sails. Explore. Dream. Discover."
- Mark Twain

We have authored this book to provide success tools for students to fast-track their careers and suggestions to educators to help successful students become even more successful. If this book helps you achieve your expectations, it will have done its job. If you put this book down feeling that you are better equipped to become a successful professional and leader, we feel that our work as authors has been accomplished.

We would appreciate your valuable feedback to make improvements to this book. You may post your feedback at http://speakermix.com/professor-m-s-rao, Facebook Page: http://www.facebook.com/pages/Professor-MSRao/ 45151651 4937414?skip_nax_wizard=true and http://speakermix.com/m-ganesh-sai or send us email: profmsr13@gmail.com and mgshyd@gmail.com. If you want information on the seminars and workshops on leadership that we conduct or our availability as speakers for your group or conference, please contact us. You may also visit our Blogs http://profmsr.blogspot.com, http://professormsrao.blogspot.com, http://professormsraoguru.

blogspot.com and http://mgshyd.wordpress.com which are read globally. These blogs pertain to Learning, Leadership, Coaching, and Soft Skills. Please post your comments directly on the blogs themselves, as it helps others appreciate your ideas. If you find the blogs interesting, please share the links with your friends, as knowledge grows when shared.

You may share your thoughts about *Soar Like Eagles! Success Tools for Freshers* on Facebook, Twitter, LinkedIn, and the websites you visit. You can also blog about it or write a book review.

We pray for your success.

Professor M.S.Rao
Founder, MSR Leadership Consultants India

M.Ganesh Sai
Founder, MGS Leadership Consultants India

About The Authors

Professor M.S.Rao,

International Leadership Guru

Blogs: http://profmsr.blogspot.com

http://professormsrao.blogspot.com

http://professormsraoguru.blogspot.com

Professor M.S.Rao is an international leadership guru who rose from humble origins. He is recognized as one of the world's leading leadership educators, authors, speakers, coaches, consultants and practitioners. He has 32 years of experience in leadership development, and conducts leadership development training programs for various corporates and educational institutions. He is a Success Coach and Motivational Speaker, and delivers guest lectures upon request. He coined a new leadership tool – *Soft Leadership Grid;*

leadership teaching tool – *11E Leadership Grid;* and innovative teaching tool – *Meka's Method.* His areas of interest include Leadership, Coaching, and Learning and Development.

He is the Founder of MSR Leadership Consultants, India and the author of 21 books including the award-winning book *21 Success Sutras for Leaders.* He has published more than 250 papers and articles in international publications such as *Leader to Leader, Leadership Excellence, T+D Magazine (ASTD), Personal Excellence, Chief Learning Officer Magazine, Emerald,* and *Sage.* He serves as an Advisor and Board Member for several prestigious international organizations including American Institute of Business Psychology (AIOBP), USA. and Global Leadership Awards, Malaysia. He has been listed as one of the leading achievers around the world in *Marquis Who's Who in the World* in 2013 - 30th Pearl Anniversary Edition. He successfully led a webinar on *Soft Leadership: A New Leadership Perspective* organized by International Leadership Association, America.

He serves on the editorial boards of various prestigious international journals including *Development and Learning in Organizations* and *Industrial and Commercial Training* of Emerald Journals - U.K, *International Journal of Business Administration* - Canada, and *Journal of Business Studies Quarterly* - USA. He is ranked as No.1 among the speakers in India as per reviews on Speakermix.org URL: http://speakermix.com/professor-m-s-rao. He can be reached at: profmsr13@gmail.com and additionally maintains three popular blogs titled 'Where Knowledge is Wealth' - URL http://profmsr.blogspot.com 'Professor M.S.Rao Born for the Students' URL http://professormsrao.blogspot.com and 'Knowledge Grows When Shared'- URL http://professormsraoguru. blogspot.com

M. Ganesh Sai, Author, India

Blog: http://mgshyd.wordpress.com

Author's Biography

M. Ganesh Sai is currently pursuing engineering education. His articles have been featured in various newspapers including *The Hindu.* He has authored 5 books including *Success Can Be Yours, Smartness Guide: Success Tools for Students, Short Stories to Share – Get Inspired*, and *Skills for Your Career Success: Touch Your Tipping Point.* His areas of interest include Success, Motivation, Leadership, and Personality Development. He is passionate about teaching, training, research and consultancy. You may see his international endorsements at: http://speakermix.com/m-ganesh-sai. He can be reached at mgshyd@gmail.com and additionally maintains a popular blog: http://mgshyd.wordpress.com.

List of Books Published by Professor M. S. Rao

1. 21 Success Sutras for Leaders
2. Smart Leadership: Lessons for Leaders
3. Success Can Be Yours
4. Spirit of Indian Youth: Soft Skills for Young Managers
5. Stand Out! Build a Successful Career and Become a Global Leader
6. Secrets of Your Leadership Success:
7. The 11 Indispensable E's of a Leader
8. Sharpen Your Mind: Acquire Tools to Achieve Your Success
9. Strategies for Improving Your Business Communication: The Book for Leaders to Communicate and Achieve Professional Success
10. Soft Leadership: Make Others Feel More Important
11. Smartness Guide: Success Tools for Students
12. Soft Skills for Students: Classroom to Corporate
13. Sage Advice for Students and Educators: Stay Inspired!
14. Soup for Academic Leaders: Acquire Teaching Tools to Achieve Your Academic Leadership Success
15. Spot Your Leadership Style: Build Your Leadership Brand
16. Secrets for Success: Failure is only a Comma, Not a Full Stop
17. Soft Skills: Enhancing Employability
18. Student Leaders: Growing from Students to CEOs